WHEN THE PERSONAL WAS POLITICAL

WHEN THE PERSONAL WAS POLITICAL

✦

Five Women Doctors Look Back

Toni Martin, M.D.

iUniverse, Inc.

New York Lincoln Shanghai

WHEN THE PERSONAL WAS POLITICAL
Five Women Doctors Look Back

iUniverse books may be ordered through booksellers or by contacting:

iUniverse
2021 Pine Lake Road, Suite 100
Lincoln, NE 68512
www.iuniverse.com
1-800-Authors (1-800-288-4677)

Because of the dynamic nature of the Internet, any Web addresses or links contained in this book may have changed since publication and may no longer be valid.

The views expressed in this work are solely those of the author and do not necessarily reflect the views of the publisher, and the publisher hereby disclaims any responsibility for them.

ISBN: 978-0-595-48726-4 (pbk)
ISBN: 978-0-595-60822-5 (ebk)

Printed in the United States of America

For Andrew, Chris and Anna

Contents

Acknowledgements

The four women in my medical school study group who signed on to this project have been generous with their time and patient over many years. (One woman, with whom we lost contact, preferred not to participate.) The other physicians I interviewed, Melvin Grumbach, Peggy Karp, Philip Lee, Deborah Wafer, John Watson, and, and the psychologist, Lillian Cartwright, also contributed valuable perspectives.

In addition to the professors mentioned above, I thank Nancy Rockafellar and Claire Brindis who read my proposal and assured me that this history was worth recording. Jane Anne Staw edited an early version of the proposal. I appreciate the members of writing groups who read excerpts, especially Debbie McCann and the late Claire Korn, who always believed I could write this book. I finished the first draft during my residency at the Mesa Refuge, a gift of time. Ramu Nagappan, Beverly Davenport and Kevin Grumbach graciously read through the final draft. I am grateful to copyeditor Rachel Trachten and cover designer Glen Ohlson, who nudged my manuscript into a book.

I thank all the people who encouraged me with words or by example during the many years I spent on this project, especially Sandra Bryson, Elizabeth Fishel, Forrest Hamer, Chris Houston, Susan Ito, Naneen Karraker, Pat Lyons, Tom McNamee, Barbara Oliver, Angelica Ramirez, Brenda Spriggs, and Maxine Turret.

Finally, I want to thank my husband and children, who let me closet myself with the computer (and write about them), even when they didn't understand why.

Preface

Over the years that I worked on this book, other writers suggested that it would be easier, and more lucrative, to write a novel or an individual memoir, than to follow the careers of five different women doctors. However, as odd as it may seem, this format is the one that fits this story. I didn't want to write a novel about women doctors: there is plenty of fantasy about us out there already. There are also personal memoirs and books of patient-centered anecdotes. I wanted to focus on us, the women doctors, as a group. As I struggled with this manuscript, it was the common themes that emerged from the juxtaposition of our lives that intrigued me. In the end, our strongest bond, stronger than that of classmates or friends, is the fact that we chose to live this social experiment, the movement of women into a male profession, together.

My friends have trusted me with intimate details of their lives, and I feel deeply honored. I made a decision not to use their real names, but they are prominent enough in their communities that they will be recognized, so their trust is all the more remarkable. I also changed the names of husbands and children. My goal was a book that was honest enough to be useful to younger women, not maximum exposure.

Finally, I have done my best to make this book as accurate as it could be. There is no intentional fiction here, but the book is based on current interviews regarding events in the past. I kept a journal, which helped anchor some events, and in the group interviews, we spoke up when our memories differed. I also returned to the library again and again, to understand the context of our lives. We couldn't remember, for example, the contraceptive controversies; we remembered the feeling of not knowing what to do.

The women in the study group reviewed the book prior to its publication. To my great relief, they offered only minor suggestions. Although I would not and could not have written this book without my friends, in the end, I am the author, and take responsibility for its shortcomings.

Introduction

When I joined the freshman class at the University of California at San Francisco School of Medicine in 1973, I was surprised and delighted to learn that we women had captured 40 of the 146 spots in the class. At the time, this number was a record for UCSF and represented one of the highest percentages of women medical students in the country. In the year 2006, UCSF is still in the forefront of female admissions, with 60 percent women in the entering class, compared to 50 percent nationwide. According to the American Medical Association, 27 percent of physicians today are women, compared to 8 percent in 1970.

Our class also had ten percent minorities and an average age of twenty-six, very old in those days when most students started their medical studies right after college. Some of our older students were returning Vietnam medics and Peace Corps volunteers. The darker, older, female students were lumped together under the heading "non-traditional" students. We represented the aftershock of three political earthquakes: the civil rights movement, the feminist movement and the Vietnam War. Even those among us who had not marched or protested and yearned to shed the "nontraditional" label knew that our presence in that class was related to forces beyond our individual endeavors. We shared a new collective consciousness.

Several years ago, I returned to my alma mater, on the volunteer clinical faculty. For a few hours each month, I served as a facilitator for a small group of students in the introductory clinical course, Foundations of Patient Care. I met with the same six medical students from their first week of school to the end of the second year. One of the explicit purposes of the group was to allow for the kind of emotional processing of experience that was discouraged when I was in medical school. The women students in my groups were at ease, lounging in class. No one had told them that they didn't belong there. They offered their opinions freely. They were not afraid that their "feminine" side would count against them. Neither were the men.

When I began to teach, I realized that my classmates and I are part of a unique generation of women doctors, sandwiched between the individual women pioneers and the women students of today who grew up with mothers in professional roles other than teaching or nursing. The pioneers were the scouts in the

1

field of medicine and we were the landing party. This is the story of how we established our beachhead and held on. We could never let down our guard, because we knew we were seen as an invading force. Today women students travel to medical school unarmed, on a passport of achievement, just like the men.

In the 1960s, when each medical school class had only a handful of women, the strategy was to be "one of the boys." Frances Conley, the Stanford neurosurgeon who wrote *Walking Out on the Boys* trained a decade before I did. She was typical of her era. She did not identify with other women (there weren't any in neurosurgery, anyway). In order to survive, she convinced herself that she was just like a man. She writes, "While I was friendly with my female classmates, we never formed true collegial relationships. We never learned to work together and support each other. I have maintained no contact with them outside of class reunions. Through subtle, unconscious social pressure, it seemed more important to be regarded as 'one of the boys' than to be seen running around with a bunch of women."

By and large, women of my generation did not want to be stereotyped by gender either. We did not view the difficulties of medical training through a pink lens. Yet as daughters of the women's movement, we understood from the beginning that gender could not be ignored. We took for granted that we would work together and we enjoyed the company of other women. We bonded like war buddies under the stress of medical school.

Like Conley, we were intent on proving how tough we were, that we could make it in the man's world of medicine. Unlike Conley, who chose not to have children, we hoped to combine the roles of mother and doctor. Perhaps because there were so many of us, we did not think of ourselves as different from other women our age. Yes, we wanted to be doctors, but as feminists we wanted everything the men had, including the families. We agreed with the author Anne Roiphe: "Feminists want good families, too. They don't want to live in dry dead places where the held hand, the shared joke, the unexpected touch never occurs."

In our youth, we did not have the imagination or the temerity to transform the workplace, only the will to persevere. We felt on probation, despite our greater numbers. Our job was to fit in, no matter what. It would be almost two decades before Anita Hill would stand up in 1991 and bring sexual harassment to the nation's attention. Our "in-between generation" was sensitized to women's issues, but confused about what our "rights" might be. One of my former classmates commented during Hill's testimony that recognizing sexual harassment for what it was, rather than just "the way things are," would have been a step up for us.

In San Francisco, the early seventies were a time of accelerated change. The medical school class before us had pressured the administration to adopt a pass-fail system by refusing to sign their names on tests. In the street, it was the height of the sexual revolution, and the wild gay bath scene set the standard for sexual self-expression. In politics, many of us endorsed "revolutionary" rhetoric and believed that we needed to develop skills to serve the community. When we closeted ourselves for intensive study, we assumed that the world of our college years, protests and free love and experiments in communal living, would be waiting for us when we emerged.

We were wrong. By the end of our training, Reagan was president, rumors of a sexually-transmitted plague were widespread, and the MBA was the degree of the hour. Lifestyle sections in the newspapers featured women who had chosen to stay home to raise their children. The backlash to feminism had begun.

Then, to our surprise, we turned out to be "women doctors." A "woman doctor" is a fine and honorable thing, but it is not the same as "a doctor." Sir William Osler, the Canadian physician who pioneered the system of bedside clinical teaching at the turn of the twentieth century, used to tease his women students by saying, "Humankind might be divided into three groups—men, women, and women physicians." A hundred years later, we are still a distinct species. Well-meaning patients have asked me, "What do you want to be called?" as though there is a separate "Ms. Doctor" title for me.

Historically, organized medicine in the U.S. excluded women, first from medical schools (many nineteenth-century women trained in Europe) and later from internships and residencies. In 1925, three-quarters of residencies approved by the American Medical Association would not consider women applicants. Without hospital training, women could not obtain the hospital privileges necessary for private practice. So women doctors founded public dispensaries for the care of women and children. Most women in medicine stayed on a separate, more public health-oriented track and did not threaten the higher-earning men.

Although the feminist movement provided the impetus for the women in our class to apply to medical school, and on some level, we assumed that a larger presence of women in medicine would lead to a more collaborative model for doctor-patient communication, we did not seek a separate female track. Our goal was a profession where the gender of the provider did not matter, and all doctors treated all people with respect. We did not consider ourselves particularly "nurturing" just because we were women, and no one else did either. In fact, our ambition was considered "masculine." The revival of the idea that women are "natural nurturers" in the wake of the psychologist Carol Gilligan's work in the 1980s caught us by surprise.

Yet the limits of approved doctor behavior were so narrow, and so masculine, we couldn't conform to them. When I was pregnant with my first child, I realized that the male "professional" stance that the psychiatrists taught us in medical school—yes, the psychiatrists taught us to interview patients—was ridiculous for someone with a belly like mine. "Never answer personal questions," the shrinks warned us. A student was reprimanded in class for answering a patient's question about whether the student's Earth shoes were comfortable. Forget it. When patients asked how far along I was, I told them. Eventually, I gave up my ambition to be "a good doctor" and settled for "a good woman doctor." In preparation for an essay I wrote for a local paper, I started to ask my friends in medicine about the "woman doctor" concept. As always, I returned to my study group, four women who were my support and reality check in medical school, and friends since. Years ago, I wrote a book, *How to Survive Medical School*, stressing the common experience. Now I was more interested in what distinguished the experience of medicine for women.

My friends were enthusiastic about this project. It still feels like we are breaking a taboo, to speak of our separateness. Their willingness to display the details of their lives, to spare others their mistakes, reminds me of the way we came together thirty years ago and examined each other to spare patients our clumsiness. I performed my first pelvic exam on a Chinese classmate who confessed to me later that it was her first intimate exam. She was more frightened of a male doctor than of a bumbling female student.

In our training, we were acutely aware of how few women role models were available. Older women doctors distanced themselves from us once they discovered we wanted to have lives as well as careers. In a sense, we served as our own role models in the group. We allowed ourselves the psychic space to experiment with different ways of being women and doctors. Like women in a communal dressing room, we tried on our women doctor identities using each other as mirrors.

At school, we tried not to call attention to the differences between women and men. Only privately, during our weekly meetings, did we dare acknowledge our fears that we would never be like the doctors who taught us. Or say out loud that we might not want to be like them. As soldiers in the trenches, we did not have the perspective to evaluate the chain of command. We focused on the light at the end of the tunnel, the autonomy we expected as practicing physicians.

As luck would have it, autonomy is in short supply in medicine nowadays. More and more, doctors work in large groups. More than 50 percent of physicians work for a salary. In groups, administrators are finding that women and men have different practice styles. Women communicate differently and provide more preventive services. Some studies find that women spend more time with patients. A few studies are even starting to show that patients have different expectations of women doctors. Yet in many ways, we resemble our male colleagues. Our suicide rate, for example, several times that of other women, even other professional women, is close to that of male doctors.

One of the questions I have asked my friends over and over in the course of our interviews is, "How do you think this experience was different for you as a woman?" Often, they shrug their shoulders and admit they don't know. As the black woman in our group, I am the double outsider, but don't know either. Sociologists who have studied gender in the workplace suggest that it does make a difference. Medical research tends to assume that the pressures on men and women at work are the same, and to focus on the impact of childbearing and motherhood on women doctors.

Unfortunately for science, we didn't live our lives with male controls. Our lives are not a study. On the other hand, three of us are married to doctors (about 50 percent of married women doctors choose doctor spouses), one to a dentist, and one to a lawyer, so we have some insight into the world of professional men. My husband and I were medical school classmates, but he had no patience for the introspection that characterized our group. I couldn't talk to him the way I could talk to my girlfriends. Our experience as women doctors at work was different from that of men before we had children, and more different once we had them.

In our lives in practice, we women physicians have straddled two racehorses of cultural change, the movement of women into traditionally male professions and the imposition of the corporate model on medicine. In the seventies, we thought of medicine as a marble temple with open pedestals for those who passed the entrance requirements. Now it appears more like a coral reef growing haphazardly in response to waves of political opinion and shifting winds of reform. Economic storms pass regularly, with mergers and downsizing in their wake. None of us imagined today's world of "managed competition" where the sands shift beneath our feet.

Every physician has made a personal accommodation to the corporate practice climate. Are the coping strategies of women different from those of men? I asked the women of my study group if they would be willing to share with me their evolution as women doctors. We took residencies in pediatrics, internal medicine, and psychiatry. Over time, one internist with a nutrition background developed a specialty in eating disorders. Another is a gastroenterologist. I am the third internist and a geriatrician. The pediatrician finished a second residency and is now an academic pediatric dermatologist. All five of us are mothers, of biological, adoptive, or stepchildren.

Three of us worked for Kaiser, a staff-model health maintenance organization often touted as an ideal situation for women physicians, although we didn't find it so. We have experimented with our hours and types of practice. One of us has never worked part time, one of us has never worked full time. One of us is a professor at our alma mater, and the rest of us have taught here and there.

We all live in California, where we have faced the cutting edge of the managed care revolution. Our experience may not be the same as that of women doctors everywhere, but trends that begin in California impact the rest of the country, for better or for worse. It is our hope that by revealing the particulars of our careers, we will provide a window into the lives of professional women of our era in general, at least the driven, self-conscious ones.

Our lives have braided many strands: the personal, the political, and the craziness of modern medicine. When we get together our conversations zigzag from new research developments to SAT prep classes to the reform of worker's compensation to family vacations. If our lives seem complicated, it's because they are. I want to convey our exhilaration and our confusion, because we rarely knew one without the other.

Our study group was a precursor to the kind of small groups that are now integrated into the curriculum. We created a safe place for ourselves because we couldn't find one in school. The medical school culture in the seventies did not acknowledge feelings. Today medical schools teach students about the role of empathy in doctor-patient communication. Medicine changed us, but we have changed medicine. In the first half of our lives in practice, we struggled to fit into systems designed for men. At that point, it felt like we had done all the changing. In the second half of our careers, we each found a different way to live in medicine, our own way. This book is an exploration of the changes on both sides.

The feminist scholar Carolyn G. Heilbrun wrote, "What became essential for women was to see themselves collectively, not individually, not caught in some individual erotic and familial plot and, inevitably, found wanting." The success of our generation of women in medicine is not only the success of those individual women, our Frances Conleys, who beat the men at their own game. As a group, we occupied the territory of medicine, changing the treatment of patients and the direction of research.

It is a joy to see men and women medical students learning in a supportive, co-operative atmosphere today. But it is simplistic to think that because there are now equal numbers of men and women medical students, there will be no differences in their experiences. Neither men nor women can shed gender roles like overcoats when they enter the hospital. Women doctors still face the question, "What does it mean to be a woman in medicine?" My generation did not feel free to ask that question out loud for fear of appearing ungrateful for our opportunity. (We were grateful. We are grateful.) We hope that our varied experience will encourage younger women who are forging their own doctor identities. What counts is that we are still here, still doctors, still women.

1. Meet the Girls

"Persevering. This adjective was endorsed by 65.6 per cent of our subjects [women medical students in the 1960s], but by only 38.3 per cent of the sample of female college students; this item was one of the most discriminating items between these two groups of women." (Lillian Cartwright, psychologist, in her PhD thesis *Women in Medicine*, 1969.)

The first time I assembled the girls at my house to talk about this project, on a Sunday afternoon, Ruth was late. The rest of us, four trim middle-aged women in nice pants and pants suits, had already assembled around the coffee table in the living room. Karen flew up from Los Angeles to join those of us in the Bay Area for this reunion. To my surprise, everyone seemed to welcome this opportunity to examine our careers.

We have been friends for thirty years now. Judith still has dark straight hair down to her waist, with bangs that fall over her eyes. The rest of us have short brown hair, Ruth and I with curls, Lorraine and Karen with waves. I am the only one who lets the gray in my hair show, and I wear glasses: the others who need them use contact lenses. Karen is the most petite. All of us work to keep fit. We dress conservatively, a lot of black, a little jewelry, usually real these days. We chat about our children until Ruth rings the bell.

When I open the door, she bursts into the conversation. "Sorry, everybody. I'm on call. I've been trying to get this surgeon to see my patient." Instantly, the energy level in the room rises from mom talk to medicine. This is not a situation that we encounter much anymore, but we've all been there.

"It makes me furious. He doesn't know me, because he's covering. I've worked all these years to show that I'm the best GI doctor in town, and he comes from elsewhere and patronizes me. If I say the patient needs to be seen today, he needs to get his ass into the hospital." Ruth is not exaggerating about her reputation. *San Francisco Focus* magazine lists Ruth, Lorraine, and Judith among the city's best doctors.

We nod in agreement. The emotion and the salty language take us back to the bad old days of medical school when we met regularly to share our exasperation. The study group was the one place we didn't have to censor ourselves, where we were sure no one would say, "You should feel lucky that you're in medical school," or "A man wouldn't get so upset."

Ruth settles down among us and I think, what a perfect way to start. Ruth is an experienced doctor in private practice. Medical etiquette and financial incentives are aligned in private practice to push the surgeon to respond. A gastroenterologist (GI specialist) is an important source of referrals for a general surgeon. Even if a surgeon doesn't think much of another doctor's clinical acumen, he doesn't argue that he doesn't need to see the patient. Not if he expects to stay in business. And a covering doctor is usually more careful not to offend referring doctors, because he has no way to judge their level of concern. Unless the referring doctor is a woman, in which case she must be overly anxious. Surely the problem can wait until Monday.

We are thirty years away from the year we started medical school. Sometimes it is difficult for us to remember what happened when. Yet the visceral feminist fire we felt then smolders in each of us, waiting for a spark.

In 1973, the campus of the University of California at San Francisco was an austere place. High on a hill, hidden in the fog, the medical school was literally an ivory tower (well, two towers) built in the 1960s. Our first year marked the hundredth anniversary of the affiliation of the campus with the University of California. The medical school, founded as the Toland School of Medicine, merged with the California School of Pharmacy and in 1873 negotiated a partnership with the University of California at Berkeley, across the San Francisco Bay. Later, nursing and dental schools were added, but the campus remained an all-health-care professional school campus, an oddity in the University of California system.

We started school the year of the Arab oil embargo, which precipitated a national energy crisis. People lined up at gas stations for fuel, and Congress imposed year-round daylight savings time to save energy. Winter quarter we had histology lab at 8 a.m., when it was still dark. Like zombies, we medical students slogged up from little flats in the Sunset and Haight Ashbury districts to Parnassus Heights, where the medical school stands. We put our weary eyes to the microscopes to study the slides of normal tissue. Anatomy and histology labs were on the eleventh floor. In the daytime, the spectacular view of San Francisco and the Bay distracted us. But those grim mornings, it could have been midnight outside.

Perhaps because there were no undergraduates, the school did not feel it needed to offer much in terms of campus life. There were two places to eat on campus, a cafeteria in the Student Union and the hospital cafeteria. The Student Union also boasted a gym, a swimming pool, and a bookstore that sold only medical books. They showed a movie on Friday nights, and there was a campus newspaper, *The Synapse*. No classes were offered aside from the professional ones. Students organized a medical Spanish class that met on campus, but didn't "count." When I returned to teach twenty-odd years later, I was more impressed with the snack shops, the flower vendor, and the bulletin boards full of notices for alternative medicine and yoga classes than I was with the new hospital.

We girls called ourselves the "study group," to differentiate us from the "women's group," which fell apart. Originally, the "women's group" membership was all the women in the class who chose to participate. In the fall of 1973, the women's movement was so much a part of our consciousness that it seemed natural to meet as soon as the class assembled. I had never been a member of a "women's group," but I had read about them for years in *Ms.* Magazine. At least twenty women crowded into a living room for the first session.

We discovered that the women's health movement had inspired most of us. I still own a copy of the original newsprint *Our Bodies, Ourselves* published by the Boston Women's Health Care Collective in 1972. Several of the women in our class had helped found the Berkeley Women's Health Collective. In lecture, most of the women sat together, as a political statement. As a black woman, I felt torn because the blacks and the Chicanos (those who identified as "people of color") also sat together. There were four other black women, but we never sat as a group. Since we sat in lecture all day eight to five except for the time we spent in labs, and Wednesday, elective day, seatmates were the core of our social life.

At first, all was well in the women's group. We took turns telling our life stories. As someone who had moved in lockstep from high school to college and then to medical school, I felt intimidated by the women with more experience. I was impressed that other women had to sacrifice family ties to pursue their dream. There was an Indian woman who walked away from an arranged marriage and a Jewish woman estranged from her Orthodox family because of her decision. It was exhilarating to get to know this group of smart, feisty women. When the wife of one of our male classmates wanted to join, we refused. She would have blown our self-congratulatory high. We didn't want to focus on relationships, but on how far we were going to go.

Some of the women in our class never joined the women's group, or left quickly when the intense political emphasis became clear. I left in the spring, after a meeting in which I felt ostracized for saying I wanted to have children. Even theoretical children were politically incorrect. The subject probably came up in the wake of my wedding announcement. Everyone knew my husband, Miles, who was a classmate. We had been college sweethearts fortunate enough to get into the same medical school. It was fine to live with him, but marriage was not cool.

Somehow, the study group emerged from the splintered women's group. We were women who enjoyed each other's company, were not politically active, and were interested in keeping the focus close to school. At the end of the first year we were just getting to know each other. We all lived close enough to walk up the hill to class. Eventually, Miles and I ended up in an apartment upstairs from Judith. Ruth and Karen shared a flat until Ruth met her husband. Later, Karen and Lorraine shared a different flat. Our world was close and intense.

It took most of the first year for our friendships to gel. I didn't invite anyone from California to my wedding, which took place in Chicago over spring vacation of first year. My parents had moved back to Chicago from Washington, D.C., where I went to high school. Neither Miles, from Connecticut, nor I, had any friends in Chicago. I did not want an engagement ring, because diamonds came from South Africa, still under apartheid rule. We had a very small wedding with relatives. So small that I made the cake, exasperated that the bakeries wouldn't take an order for a wedding cake that only served twenty-five. So small that my sister-in-law asked if I were pregnant. Scandal was the only reason she could imagine avoiding a large celebration. We spent one night at a famous downtown hotel, The Palmer House, for our honeymoon. We couldn't afford room service, so my Miles went out for McDonald's.

When we flew back to California, we were flat broke. The girls came over the week we returned and brought us an electric coffee grinder as a wedding present, one that we used for twenty-five years. I remember thinking for the first time that these were my girlfriends, not just classmates. Looking back, the coffee grinder seems symbolic of the life we had all moved to San Francisco to achieve, a life where gourmet coffee beans were available (this is 1974, remember) and we could afford to buy them.

Our weekly meetings rotated among our apartments, all decorated with secondhand furniture and overflowing with heavy medical books. We practiced physical exams on each other, experimenting with ophthalmoscopes and stethoscopes. We reviewed for tests, which were constant. On the quarter system, midterms and finals seemed only a few weeks apart. We studied for part one of the National Boards, which came in June of the second year. When we started on the hospital wards, in July of that year, we kept meeting, comparing notes from our clinical experience. Miles and Judith's husband, Bob, banished to the bedroom during our turns to host, complained that we couldn't be working because they heard giggling all evening.

Over the years, there were tears as well as laughter. During the clinical years of training, we clung to each other for support. We didn't want to share our feelings of inadequacy and loneliness with our male classmates because they would interpret them as weakness. My husband, often as stressed as I was, wanted to "leave it at the office." Recent research suggests that women and men may have different biological responses to stress. The "flight or fight" response we have been taught is "normal" is the male response to the adrenalin and testosterone cocktail their bodies release. Women release adrenalin and oxytocin, the same hormone that controls milk letdown in breast-feeding. Psychologist Laura Cousino Klein believes the oxytocin causes a "tend and befriend" response. It is ironic to think that at the same time we were arguing that biology was not destiny, we women might have been responding to our hormones when we bonded together. On the other hand, we may have huddled together because we felt powerless.

We called ourselves "the girls" partly because we rejected the p.c. "women," and partly in self-conscious parody of the idea of women at leisure we'd absorbed growing up. Our mothers had all worked during most of our childhoods, but through TV and magazines we knew the world of ladies who lunched. According to the press hype at the time, our generation of women broke ground by working, as though all women in the fifties and sixties were the suburban housewives of "*Leave It to Beaver*"and" *Father Knows Best.*" In fact, it was the choice of a traditionally male profession that crossed the boundary of our mothers' generation. All of our mothers except mine were teachers. My mother had helped my father edit *The Chicago Daily Defender*, the black newspaper in Chicago.

If only we had recorded our discussions back then, we might be able to summon up the answer to the question that obsesses us now: "Why?" Why did we choose such an arduous path? We knew it would be long and hard, even if we didn't find out how hard until later. We knew that we wouldn't have the glory of the pioneer.

From the perspective of the new century, when my children's idea of a successful career is to make a killing in stocks or software and retire at thirty, it does seem rather old-fashioned to train for a career that doesn't even start until that age. All I can say is that I felt less different from other women then than I do now. We were moving with a high-achieving cohort of women, and we were determined not to let our sex define us. Most of the women I knew were pursuing graduate degrees or traveling. When my first child was born, and I joined a mothers group (briefly), I was surprised to find myself by far the most educated.

At the first group book interview, I asked the "girls" if they, too, felt more different now than ever. To my surprise, they said yes, but the way they felt different was that they felt younger than other women their age. Looking around the table, I thought we looked well-preserved, but I knew affection might be clouding my vision. In my research, I've learned that we women doctors exceed all the recommendations for preventive health care in our own lives. We don't smoke, we eat low-fat foods, we exercise, we remember our sunscreen. Appearance aside, we spent our twenties (in Judith's case her thirties) in a deep freeze of training and emerged to start work and family in our thirties. Retirement seems far away when college tuition is due.

I will start our individual portraits with Ruth, because medical school is a place where it is important to be smart and quick, and she is both. She majored in Social Relations in college, deciding to apply to medical school so late that she had to take an extra year of pre-med requirements. Yet she ranked second in our medical school class. We all hoped that she would pull ahead of the guy who held number one. She has the fast delivery of a native New Yorker, and an astonishing fund of information. In an interesting coincidence, Lorraine's husband Sam met Ruth when he was a medical student and she was his resident on the medicine clerkship. "She was incredibly competent and smart," Sam reports, "a great role model for me." He remembers what pleasure Ruth took in formulating a long differential diagnosis, a list of possible diseases that fit the patient's symptoms and examination. He says, in retrospect, that he didn't appreciate at the time how remarkable the experience was, since it was his first clerkship.

I asked Ruth once how she managed to study so much, since she told us she was frequently depressed and very homesick the first year. "When I'm depressed, I study," she answered. To help her concentrate, she used a white noise generator to filter out extraneous sound. She told me about the white noise generator in anatomy lab, where we shared a cadaver.

One of the first social tasks we faced as medical students was to divide ourselves into groups of four, so that each group could be assigned a cadaver. For the first time in history, there were two all-women groups in the class. Ruth, Judith, and I joined another woman. Lorraine was a member of the other all-women group, along with Ally, the member of the study group who declined to participate in this book. Only Karen, who took anatomy over the summer before the first year, worked with men. It's hard to remember now why the all-women groups were such a big deal, but they were. The men didn't like it.

I already knew I felt more comfortable studying with women. Studying with my husband was out of the question—he is the hare to my tortoise, although often as not, he would earn the better grade. In a physics course one summer, I had two lab partners, a man and a woman. The woman worked as I did, methodically, following the instructions. If the circuit didn't work, we would check each connection individually to find the problem. The guy would try to tear the whole thing down and start over. Luckily, it was two against one.

Judith's husband took pictures of us in anatomy lab. We're not posing for the camera; we are intent on our work. Our cadaver was like another member of our group. We named her, but we can't remember her name, only the name I vetoed: "Gertrude." It is my mother's name. We were not told anything about our cadaver. Two afternoons a week, for an entire school year, we dissected her skinny body. Eventually we discovered that her lungs were riddled with cancer. Before examinations, we would return to the lab on weekends and at night to seek her help.

Although she was a Harvard graduate, Ruth was the queen of academic insecurity. It took the rest of us a while to figure out that if she was moaning that she hadn't had a chance to study at all, it meant she'd taken a break for dinner. Or that if she left a test worrying about her grade, it might be as low as an A minus. This can be an obnoxious trait, but Ruth's anxiety was so obviously genuine, we couldn't hold it against her. We did stop listening, though.

Ruth's father was the foreman of a textile mill in Johnston, South Carolina, when she was a baby. Their family was one of two Jewish families in town. When her father integrated the labor force, in accordance with his communist philosophy, the Ku Klux Klan burned a cross on their lawn. Her mother was so miserable in the South that the family moved back to New York City. Eventually, her father inherited a women's underwear factory from his uncle, but in the early years, money was scarce. Ruth's mother went back to school after her second son was born (Ruth is the oldest) and started teaching elementary school to help make ends meet. When she started school, Ruth contributed 25 cents a week to a savings account. In second grade, her parents raided her account to pay bills.

Ruth married a doctor she met on her first clinical rotation in medical school, and they have two boys. We girls in the area attended the Bar Mitzvahs of her two sons. I remember her at the first one, where she was radiant, dancing in higher heels than any sensible woman doctor would wear. Her husband referred to her as "Doctor Ruth" in his speech at the reception, and Ruth herself touched on what she called "the experiment of our generation," combining fulltime careers and motherhood. Over the years, we had shared her struggle to find a balance between child rearing and our profession. We knew, more than anyone in the room outside her family, how much angst lay behind that happy moment.

Karen, Ruth's former roommate, is a California girl from Los Angeles. She and her younger brother grew up in Culver City, where her dad ran a liquor store and her mother was a substitute teacher. As a teenager, she decorated her room with the lighted signs her father brought home to her. At her high school, only about 20 percent of the students went on to four-year colleges, and she remembers what a pleasure it was to find more serious students at the University of California at Berkeley, across the San Francisco Bay from our medical school. Karen had long hair when we entered medical school, and superficially seemed more like a flower child than a professional. Her speech was full of "gee" and "kinda" and pauses to think things over. Some women intimidated the guys in our class, but Karen's soft-spoken style made everyone feel comfortable. She was as popular with the men as with the women. Karen was the only one of us who took the option to start anatomy the summer before first year, so she helped orient us when we arrived.

At the first group interview in my living room, Karen told us that she was an English major for a year, until she decided that she couldn't spend her life criticizing other people's work. I remember her curled up with a novel, when she had a chance, or hiking. When Karen gravitated toward psychiatry in medical school, it seemed like a perfect fit because there was always a dreamy, contemplative quality about her. Only recently did I learn that she majored in medical physics in college and first approached psychiatry as an undergraduate through the biochemistry of schizophrenia. She also volunteered at the emergency room of the county hospital on weekend nights while she was in college. Karen recalls that she felt her boyfriend at the time, an intern, was grappling with "big questions" and she liked that. She shrugs as she talks about the awards she won as an undergraduate, saying "I was always good in science."

Now Karen divides her time between a part-time practice of occupational psychiatry and a busy household of girls. The three older stepchildren who were teenagers when she married their father are out of the house. Her own three younger girls are the teenagers now. Her husband, a dentist who owned a chain of dental clinics, is retired. Since her practice is in Los Angeles, she frequently uses the Spanish she learned traveling in Central America. Although I have never seen her play tennis, which has become her passion, it is on the tennis court that I imagine her today, tan and graceful.

Later in medical school, when Ruth met her husband to be, Karen roomed with Lorraine. Lorraine's medical school career started with tragedy. She had a turbulent college education, at three different schools, with a stint as a full-time political organizer and commune member in Seattle in between. Her mother died of leukemia. Finally she ended up at Boston University, taking pre-med courses. She decided that if she did well, she would be a doctor; if not, she would be a nurse. To her surprise, she aced the science courses and was admitted to UCSF. When she flew home to Los Angeles to spend a week before school started, all her relatives except her father were assembled at the airport to greet her. "I knew immediately," she says. Her father had died of a heart attack. A month later she had to walk into the anatomy lab and dissect a cadaver who had died the same month.

I remember Lorraine driving the 1965 Dodge Dart she inherited from her father, calculating how long the money he had left her would last. (She stretched it as far as she could: she even found a recipe for chicken gizzards that she tried out on her roommates.) Her father was a lawyer, but not a big money lawyer. He finished law school when he was forty and set up a solo practice. Originally, he and Lorraine's mother were labor organizers with the Communist party. One of her mother's factory jobs was to x-ray O'Henry candy bars to make sure there were no foreign objects inside. Lorraine has always wondered if that job could have contributed to her mother's leukemia and early death. Lorraine was born in Oakland, but the family moved to Los Angeles when Lorraine was in junior high school. She never felt Southern California was home.

Her parents left the Communist party after the revelations about Stalin in the mid-fifties. When her father went back to law school (he had finished one year after college), her mother studied for a teaching credential in special education. She was afraid of the blacklist and reasoned that no one would care who was teaching the mentally retarded. For a while, their grandparents supported the family. As a treat, their parents would take them to eat in the Student Union, the fanciest restaurant they could afford.

Lorraine is the second of four children, sandwiched between her older sister, "the Beauty," and the only boy. It was not an easy spot. She did well in school, but she was not the all-round star her sister was and never felt as close to her mother. Yet she has an infectious self-confidence. A nephew, her older sister's son, who lived with Lorraine's family for a few months, talks about the forthright way she approaches household problems, whether about plumbing or scheduling. He says she starts from the idea "I ought to be able to figure this out." At one point in medical school when I despaired about the road ahead, she told me that she had taken enough sociology courses to know that it was just a matter of hanging tough, that it was not the material but our social position that was difficult. She was right.

Today she is a pediatric dermatologist at UCSF, with a worldwide reputation. Her combination of scholarship and good sense make her a wonderful teacher. She met her husband, also an academic physician, on her first job at Kaiser Hospital. She was the last among us to marry, only to find that her biological clock had run out early. So she adopted twins, a characteristically bold move.

A few years ago, Lorraine traded in a business class ticket to Argentina for two coach tickets, and took me along with her to a pediatric dermatology conference in Cordoba. I see her standing at the lectern, the honored expert from los Estados Unidos, describing her research in Spanish to dermatologists from all over South America.

Judith was older than the rest of us, with a career as a nutritionist and a marriage behind her. Her waist-length hair was her signature, then and now, along with her super-healthy diet. We laughed when she admitted that even her children eat fast food at times. There was something mysterious about Judith at first. Slowly the stories emerged, about the alcoholic ex-husband who was a Navy man, the work counseling low-income black women (she knew as much about soul food as I did), the new fiance, a lawyer she had met on the East Coast. Today Judith tells us that she had to move to Washington, D.C. from the Virginia suburbs to get a divorce without accusing her husband of adultery.

She met her second husband in 1970 when they were both working in Washington. Judith was a dietician in a public clinic, and Bob was working for the Office of Economic Opportunity, surveying resources in poor black neighborhoods. When Judith walked into the grocery store to buy sardines for lunch, he felt he had to include her in his interview sample because she was the first white person he had seen in days.

Her wedding was in September of 1974. Ruth attended the outdoor ceremony in Washington, D.C. Judith couldn't tell her husband's Orthodox Jewish grandparents that she was divorced. It was bad enough that she was not Jewish and was eight years older than her husband. They chose vegetarian food for their wedding, catered by the Golden Temple of Conscious Cookery, but the kosher grandparents wouldn't eat it. The couple honeymooned in Nova Scotia in a motel so cheap that the owners also sold night crawlers to get by. Judith remembers hearing the fishermen early in the mornings and seeing worms in her dreams.

Although she had set medicine as her eventual goal as early as 1965, Judith detoured for an MPH in nutrition. She roomed with a first-year medical student when she studied to be a dietician. She was intrigued by her roommate's bone box, the assortment of bones first year students borrow to study skeletal anatomy at home. When she told her husband that she was thinking of medicine, he told her that his woman could not have more degrees than he did. A native Californian, she had followed him east to CIA "spy school." When she left him in 1969, she started to take the physics and mathematics classes she needed to qualify for admission to medical school. Her only sister, who was sixteen months younger than Judith, died of a brain tumor at UCSF in August of 1970, a few weeks after Judith met Bob. Her resolve to enter medical school solidified during her sister's illness.

Like Lorraine's mother and father, Judith's parents were also Communists. Her father was an architect, her mother the director of a preschool. Once while her mother was visiting her parents' grave in a cemetery in Glendale, two men came up to her and urged her into a car. One was an FBI agent, the other a parent at the preschool she directed. They told Judith's mother that if she denounced her husband, she could keep her job. Although the marriage was rocky, already headed for the divorce that came a few years later, her mother courageously replied, "If I get a divorce, it won't be for you." She was fired and never able to get another teaching job. Judith, too, remembers hard times, represented by one pair of "ugly brown shoes" each September that had to last until the following school year.

While some of the older medical students chafed at their demotion from independent adult to apprentice, Judith seemed to take it in stride. She offered her knowledge of nutrition and clinical experience as resources for the rest of us to draw on, but she was always our peer, not our older sister. She and I became mothers within a month of each other. Judith also adopted children because an infection from a Dalkon Shield IUD left her infertile. Another sign of the times.

A few years ago, Judith closed her primary care practice and took a salaried position at an alternative medical clinic. She counsels people with serious medical illnesses like cancer and AIDS, using both her medical and nutritional expertise. She grins widely as she announces, "I can spend as much time with a patient as I want!" Best of all, there is no night call and no ongoing patient responsibility. She is no one's regular doctor anymore.

Judith and her younger son once took a working eco-vacation in Bolivia together. Sitting on my sofa, she tosses her hair back and chortles as she describes her phone call to her husband when the week was over. "He asked if we had fun," she gasps. "The conditions were very primitive, the heat was relentless, the workday was long. 'Fun' was the last word I would use." When Judith attended her

45th high school reunion at Pasadena High, she received a round of applause as the only woman doctor out of a class of 847.

Of the group, I am the one who has flitted about the most, making two major job transitions to everyone else's one. I have also developed a parallel career, writing for newspapers and magazines. When I came to medical school, I was as clueless as everyone else. Although I had majored in geology at Harvard, I did not feel confident as a scientist. On the other hand, I felt "buffeted by the times," as Ruth put it. I was a privileged middle-class black woman, the middle child in a family of five girls, expected to do something significant with my life. I could "do science," which was considered a talent in itself. Medicine was a politically acceptable way to do it, since it meant helping people. Geology was not.

My father had moved on from the *Chicago Defender* to a political post in Washington, D.C., as deputy secretary of the Democratic National Committee. He worked with Presidents Kennedy, Johnson, and Carter. Although definitely not a Communist (he once had a fit when my older sister started to sing the union song "Joe Hill") my father could not get a security clearance to work in the White House in the early sixties because he had been a champion of the black union movement in Detroit. J. Edgar Hoover still had his death grip on the FBI then. The background check for my father's position in the Carter White House reached as far as our neighbors in San Francisco. They told the FBI that I was a medical student, and that I studied all the time.

When Ruth described her choices at the end of college, I laughed in agreement because her predicament was precisely the same as mine. "There I was, at the end of college at Harvard and Radcliffe, surrounded by graduate students in the arts and sciences who had been there for ten years, trying to write their theses, completely unable to, living in filthy apartments, and I thought, 'I don't think that I can do this. I need something that's a little more solid and concrete and focused in my life.'"

I had also fallen in love with the man I married, who always wanted to be a doctor. We applied to UCSF as a long shot, because we had both enjoyed a summer we had spent in California (separately). We expected to end up in New York City, since there were several medical schools there, and our chances of both getting in somewhere were higher.

At first glance, I seem to be the odd woman out in a group of Jewish, or (in Judith's case Jewish by marriage), women. But I had always studied with Jewish girls. My parents sent me to private schools, and in those days of de facto segregation, only schools founded by Jews, or friendly to Jews, would admit black students. Except for the two years of junior high school I spent in an Episcopal school, I sang Hanukkah songs every year. I thought most white people were Jewish until seventh grade. During the Civil Rights movement, Jews and blacks marched side by side. In retrospect, that moment of cultural solidarity passed quickly, as the prep schools desegregated and politics in the Middle East drove a wedge between blacks and Jews, but the moment marked me.

If I had sought friendships only with the black women in my class, I would have been in trouble. We had a high attrition rate. By the time our study group coalesced, at the end of the first year, one black woman had dropped out for academic reasons, another had developed lupus and required extended medical leave. (She is well and practicing today.) A third woman dropped out second year to have a baby. (She returned two years later.) Only two of us graduated on time.

After a stint in private practice and at Kaiser, I ended up working exclusively in the hospital for five years. I am a general internist with additional credentials in geriatrics. Now, I live the freelance life. I am a medical disability consultant two days a week in the regional office of Social Security, I work one afternoon a week at the Berkeley Primary Care Clinic, and I write. Like Judith, I am no one's regular doctor. A visitor looking for me at home would find me in my study, a room carved out of the garage. I write at a desk with a wall of books behind me and the garden in front of me.

There have been many meetings at my house since that first meeting and many calls to Los Angeles to fill in Karen's part of the story. That first day we focused on our decision to enter medical school. We all felt that we were a generation set apart by political forces, particularly the women's movement. Lorraine, the ex-activist, called it "a time when polarization and contentiousness was considered the norm in society." The fact that we came from political families and were inspired by feminism, yet dropped out of the women's group because it was too confrontational, is a measure of the intensity of sentiment in our class. Karen remarked that her stepchildren never think of changing the world, the way we did. Of course, we had seen the world change in the sixties, so we knew it could be done. Our children are considerably more affluent than we were, too. "Not so hungry," Lorraine notes.

We were not looking for "a profession." Only Ruth even considered law school as an option; all of us were attracted to the intellectual content of medicine. Ruth was dating a third-year medical student, and remembers his roommates talking about antibodies. Three of us were dating someone heading for medicine when we made our decision, and Judith's roommate initially sparked her interest. Lorraine did not have a friend in the same role, but she was looking for a job, not a career, when she initially opted for nursing. She admits she thought medicine probably only required a year or so beyond nursing when she decided to take the pre-med sciences. Lillian Cartwright, a psychologist who studied women medical students at UCSF in the sixties found that almost half of them didn't consider medical school until they were in college. A study of male medical students about the same time found that 86 percent of them had thought about medicine before college.

Looking back, it is as though we were all sitting in a waiting room at an airport, preparing to board a domestic flight, and the women's movement came along and offered us a ticket to a foreign country. All we had to do was pass a test to show that we were smart enough to learn the language. We didn't know much about that country, but the women we spoke to assured us that once we learned the language, we would be respected and powerful citizens, with skills to care for people. It was a land of vast intellectual territory, with cliffs of knowledge to scale and unexplored caves of mystery and vista points that overlooked the whole of human experience. It was a little scary, because we didn't know people there, but previously women who wanted to go had to fight for a place on the airplane. The women's movement had struggled to obtain the tickets, and if we turned them down, younger women might not be offered the same opportunity. We took the tickets.

Ruth said that she knew if she put herself in front of a book for long enough she could pretty much learn anything. Lorraine cracked, "We can vouch for that," and we all giggled. None of us had doctors as parents or close family. Except for Ruth, whose brother is a doctor, we were the only ones in our families to choose medicine. Our ignorance probably helped keep us from getting discouraged. Would we do it all over again, knowing what we know now? The psychiatrist Anna Fels, a woman of our generation, asks herself the same question in her book about women and ambition. "Would I do this training again? I'm not sure. I love being a doctor, but at that historical moment becoming a woman physician was a brutal, confusing, and often demoralizing process." Amen.

My friends and I agree that it has been a great adventure, but we are glad that no one has to repeat our experience. As Judith put it, "The self-assertiveness I learned was worth the price of admission." We think of Ruth arguing with the surgeon to see her patient emergently. In medicine, men learn to size up a situation, act, move on. Women of our generation learned to size up a situation, act, defend the action against the men who questioned it, and move on. That's assertiveness training.

2. The Seventies, Our Cultural Context

"During the first 65 years of the twentieth century, about one American marriage in twenty ended in divorce. Since 1980, more than two marriages out of every five—nearly half—have ended in divorce." (David Frum, *How We Got Here: The Seventies, the Decade that Brought You Modern Life,* 2000)

In January 1970, Lorraine, aged twenty, joined five men and one other woman in a "sixties suburban" house in a working-class neighborhood near Seattle. They spent their days organizing students at the University of Washington and meeting with other political collectives, like the Weathermen, who were not yet underground. The habits of the men annoyed the two women: the men never cleaned up after themselves and brought home random women for sex.

One day, it was raining (it was always raining) and the biggest slob in the house, a nineteen year old with long frizzy hair and a paunch, drove Lorraine back from a meeting. He pulled into a burger joint for a snack and asked her if she wanted anything. No, she didn't. It annoyed her that he would spend money on fast food when members of the collective posed as indigents to obtain the food stamps sitting on a shelf in their kitchen. Plus, she was trying to eat less meat, as a step toward a healthier and more politically correct diet. She watched him stretch his mouth around a double burger.

"You shouldn't eat that stuff," she said.

He chewed. "What difference does it make what I eat? We're all going to die in two years anyway, when the revolution comes."

She didn't answer, but she thought about what he had said. She did not believe that she would be dead in two years, or that the revolution was imminent. Years later, she told us, "It was the beginning of the end of my life as a political activist."

A year and a half later, on the other side of the country, I woke one morning at 5 a.m., pulled on my clothes, and left the warmth of my dorm room at Radcliffe to follow my roommate out into the cold, dark morning. She started her car, a VW bug, and we drove across the river into Boston. Our destination was Roxbury, the black ghetto, where we joined a group of Black Panthers and other volunteers to cook breakfast in a school cafeteria. The cafeteria was a cavernous room, still dark. The light from the open kitchen door in the back was enough to allow us to navigate around the long, laminated tables with the benches attached. My roommate laughed and joked with the other people while we mixed pancake batter and defrosted orange juice. I didn't know anyone else because it was my first time. But I am rarely jolly at 6 a.m.

The kids started to arrive a little before seven. Not that many it seemed to me, and not that hungry. At least I remember leftover food. There was something depressing about watching children eat breakfast in that institutional setting. Bottles of syrup did not belong on those tables. Ketchup and mustard, yes. Syrup, no. I did not come away feeling proud that I had helped give power to the people, the way my roommate did. I felt tired and out of sorts.

The next time my roommate asked me to go with her, we had an argument. I felt she was always pushing me to be more radical than I was. "Either I can pass organic chemistry or I can help the Free Breakfast Program. I can't do both," I screamed. She ended up withdrawing from school after that semester, retreating home to figure out whether she wanted to be a student or a political activist. Eventually, she returned to her studies, but she graduated from college the same year I graduated from medical school. Recently, she shared with me the poem, "To Those Born Later" by Bertolt Brecht, words she lived by in college. I was struck by the sentence, "Oh, we who wanted to prepare the ground for friendliness could not ourselves be friendly."

It is hard to remember, even for us, how politically charged our lives were in those days. For four of us, college life was dominated by the Vietnam War. After the protests about the bombing of Cambodia in 1970, many campuses, including Harvard, closed down and sent students home without final exams. This was a bewildering end to my freshman year. Our male classmates faced the draft. Our campuses hosted demonstration after demonstration. Judith also lived with constant demonstrations in Washington, D.C. Every day we made decisions about when and how to participate.

We knew people who dropped out of school to join the Panthers or Bubba Free John or who ran away to communes in Vermont or Northern California. My husband participated in a building takeover in college. He had a macrobiotic friend who drank only carrot juice for months. One friend lost her Angolan husband in that country's civil war. Another friend lost his wife in the Greensboro,

South Carolina, massacre. It was a time when people put themselves in harm's way.

Although we never talked about it, the five of us who ended up in the study group were not comfortable with direct political action. None of us liked the idea of relinquishing control of our lives to some charismatic leader, political or dietary. In a sense, studying science released us from the burden of deciding on a day-to-day basis which demonstration to attend, because we didn't have time. The labs required for science courses kept us off the streets.

In medical school we didn't have the time to follow politics at all. It was okay, because we were gaining skills that we could use in the service of a transformed society. We accepted the drudgery of medical school while our friends from college were tripping around the world because we believed that we would burst forth as new doctors for a new day. We were inspired by barefoot doctors in China and midwives in Appalachia. We studied medical Spanish from the text, *Donde No Hay Doctor* (Where There Are No Doctors). My husband used to quote Mao Tse-tung: "The test of a horse is a long journey, the test of a man is a difficult task. The only way out is to work hard and serve the people."

Much of our experience of medical school was shaped by being in San Francisco, at UCSF. Dr. John Watson, a biochemist who served as UCSF Dean of Admissions in the 1970s refers to that time as "years of ferment." Watson, who believed that doctors on the admissions committee accepted students in their own image, molded a diverse committee that rapidly increased the number of women and minority students in the entering classes. In 1973, many medical schools still had only a handful of women and underserved minorities. They were reluctant to consider students who weren't coming straight from college. UCSF was ahead of the times.

UCSF's position at the vanguard is all the more remarkable because there was little student agitation on campus in the 1960s to press for change. In fact, it was a group of black employees (including janitors and clerks), not students, who formed the Black Caucus in the 1960s. The Black Caucus lobbied the administration to admit more minority students, under an affirmative action plan. They found a receptive climate on campus, partly because the 1960s were a time of expansion for the University of California in general. Three new medical schools and three new campuses were founded. When the pie is enlarging, it is less difficult to find a piece for the newcomers.

There was no "Women's Caucus" on campus to lobby for women, as the Black Caucus did for minority students. No one had a stake in our success. When I asked Dr. Watson why the number of women in the classes kept rising, he felt it had as much to do with the rise in applications as with any change in attitude on the campus. While minority applicants sometimes lacked the traditional measures of undergraduate success, so that the admissions committee looked for other signs of promise, the women applicants usually excelled in their courses and aced the standardized tests. Conservative faculty members could not argue that women would not be able to compete in medical school, the way they tried to argue against minority students. Of course, the minority students proved them wrong as well.

In addition to the new kinds of students, there was a new culture emerging within the faculty. We noticed that some of the junior faculty in the basic sciences wore jeans as we did, and seemed very approachable, although they worked like fiends. Once we reached the wards in the third year, we didn't see any more of this group. It turns out that these younger guys were the molecular biologists, who brought a more casual culture to the medical sciences, in much the same way that the dot-commers brought a more casual culture to business.

The molecular biologists were mainly in the lab, but we met a few of them as section leaders. We didn't know what to make of them. Sometimes they were hard to follow in class, and we didn't understand their passion for research. Most of our teachers force fed us facts but didn't ask us to think. They were PhD professors who considered themselves true scientists and were scornful of medical students. They felt we only wanted to apply science to make money. The molecular biologists were different. They seemed to care whether we understood their medical frontier. Only when two of those young men, Harold Varmus and Michael Bishop, shared the Nobel Prize in 1989 for the discovery of the oncogene did we understand just how different they were.

One of Lorraine's section leaders was Herb Boyer. In contrast to Varmus and Bishop, he seemed bored in class and unenthusiastic about teaching. It turned out that he had other things on his mind. In 1976, the same year Varmus and Bishop made their discovery, Boyer founded Genentech, thereby launching the biotechnology industry. Using the recombinant DNA technique Boyer had pioneered, Genetnech announced in 1978 that they had cloned human insulin. The balance of power in the medical world listed from the East Coast to the West Coast as UCSF attracted more attention and research dollars. In 1972, when I told my pre-med advisor at Harvard that I was considering UCSF, he admitted that he had hardly heard of the place. A decade later, the molecular biologists, biotechnology, and sadly, AIDS, had put UCSF on the medical map.

Other inventions of the early seventies had a dramatic impact on our practice lives. In 1973, the technology of the computerized axial tomography, or the CAT scan, emerged in medicine. When we started on the wards in 1975, the neurologists were just learning what an amazing tool the CAT scan of the brain could be. Before the CAT scan, neurologists performed long detailed examinations of patients to answer the question, "Where's the lesion?" when a patient presented with a stroke or a brain tumor. There was a nuclear medicine brain scan, which might give a vague idea of where the problem was, but if a neurosurgeon needed to know exactly where to operate, he would have to order an angiogram. The angiogram, or injection of dye into the arteries of the head, carried a small risk of death and a significant risk of stroke. It was not a test anyone ordered just to confirm a clinical impression. A CAT scan without dye, on the other hand, was as safe as a chest x-ray and could show exactly where in the brain the problem lay. One neurologist told me sadly, "The CAT scan took all the fun out of neurology."

If the CAT scan didn't show the lesion, the other imaging study invented in the early seventies, the nuclear magnetic resonance scan, or MRI, would. In our practice lives, we have watched these studies revolutionize imaging of the entire body. Surgeons used to routinely perform an "exploratory" operation when a patient presented with abdominal pain. In other words, they opened up the abdomen to look for the problem. Today they order a CAT scan or an MRI or ask a stomach specialist to take a look up and down the gastrointestinal tract with a flexible tube, another technology that boomed in the seventies.

The first personal computers also hit the market in the mid-seventies. Male doctors my age had not learned to type in school. Many women hadn't either, afraid they would end up secretaries. None of us would have guessed that we would all be keyboarding by the end of the century as our hospitals threatened us with the specter of the paperless chart. Doctors of our generation have adapted to technology as best we can, some kicking and screaming, some diverted from the practice of medicine entirely to design medical software. In our group, Lorraine and I are the "early adapters," she because of the demands of academia, me because of the demands of editors.

A final medical development of the 1970s was the use of healing therapies outside the Western medical model. In 1971, a reporter for the *New York Times*, James Reston, who accompanied President Nixon to China, underwent an emergency appendectomy there. Acupuncture was used for anesthesia and pain control. His story piqued the nation's interest in this exotic therapy. In 1973, the American Medical Association grandly declared that the practice of acupuncture, thousands of years old, was an experimental medical practice.

Suddenly all sorts of healing traditions—herbs, homeopathy, spinal manipulation, and some not so traditional, like mega-vitamin therapy—became trendy. At first these were called "alternative therapies." As medical students, we lobbied to learn more about nutrition in our curriculum. We were disappointed when the nutritionists imported from U.C. Berkeley showed us that there was no data to support the use of Vitamin C to prevent or cure the common cold. They taught us about calories and how scientists arrived at the minimum daily requirements for vitamins, not particularly exciting topics.

Today the preferred term is "complementary medicine," a change that indicates how much the medical establishment has had to accommodate these therapies and their practitioners. My medical students are taught to ask patients what herbs they might be taking and to respect these other traditions. Some of us deal with populations in which patients only seek our help when their complementary therapies fail. Lorraine describes mothers who wince when they hear the words "hydrocortisone cream," as though she is prescribing topical poison.

When we were medical students, we were marginally aware of the cutting-edge research at UCSF. Closer to our world were the reverberations of the sexual revolution and the human potential movement that were felt on campus. San Francisco in the seventies was ground zero for a new sexual tolerance. In 1973, the year we started medical school, the Board of Trustees of the American Psychiatric Association (APA) removed homosexuality from the second edition of the *Diagnostic and Statistical Manual of Mental Disorders* (DSM II). This action was a direct response to gay activism. A few years before, when the APA met in San Francisco, protesters had picketed and disrupted sessions.

The DSM is the reference work that therapists turn to for the classification of mental disease. In DSM I, homosexuality was a "Sociopathic Personality Disturbance." People in this category did not have to experience psychological distress to have a problem: they were ill because they were not "in conformity with the prevailing cultural milieu." When we arrived in San Francisco, there was a flourishing gay community and a few members of our class were out of the closet. We women felt a certain kinship with the many gay patients we saw. Like us, they had been denied the right to declare their sexuality on their own terms. In 1973, feminists celebrated *Roe v. Wade*, the Supreme Court decision that upheld a woman's right to an abortion, the same way gay activists celebrated the change in the DSM. Sex didn't have to be about procreation.

If walking the streets of the gay Castro district left any doubt in our minds about sexual liberation, our mandatory sex course convinced us that we had entered a brave new world. The centerpiece of the sex course was a movie presentation called "*The Fuckarama,*" which took place downtown at the San Francisco Museum of Erotic Art (now defunct). We lounged on pillows while hours of sexually explicit films played on three screens. Back on campus, there were lectures about sexuality from a spectrum of people whose voices were emerging in the sexual arena: gay, transgender, disabled.

Then there were the sections, taught by sex therapists. In these small groups, we were encouraged to talk about our own sex lives and sexual hang-ups, sort of mandatory group therapy with people we knew all too well. My husband and I made a pact to keep our mouths shut in section. The therapists didn't care. They acted as though the few of us who were married were mildly retarded. When we matured, we would divorce and have multiple partners. Yet even those of us who were married were caught up in the sexual euphoria of that fleeting moment between the introduction of the pill and the recognition of AIDS. It was our honeymoon, after all.

Many of our professors had divorce on their minds. It was clear that some of them envied our generation's more relaxed attitude toward sex and wished they had been born later. (A few were predatory. An intern killed herself in the wake of an affair with a professor.) In fact, the percentage of Americans in their forties who were married dropped from 84 percent in 1972 to 67 percent in 1982. *Fear of Flying* by Erica Jong, a celebration of the "Zipless Fuck" (sex between strangers) was at the top of the fiction bestseller lists in 1974. "Smash monogomy!" cried the Weathermen.

As women in medical school, we were supposed to be emblematic of the new, sexually liberated woman. "A woman without a man is like a fish without a bicycle" was a popular slogan. According to the media, women like us were striding fearlessly into the future, putting self-fulfillment before family, like Meryl Streep in *Kramer vs. Kramer,* the divorce movie of the decade. Yet none of us felt that way. Judith, Ruth, and I married in medical school. Lorraine and Karen saw dating as a way of finding a life partner, not as a permanent lifestyle.

It is true that we were not interested in the "traditional" family, in which Dad maneuvers in the world and Mom keeps house, but living alone and having orgies on the weekend didn't appeal to us either. Mary Richards, the single career woman played by Mary Tyler Moore on her show, was more our speed. She was a "good girl" who worked hard and had sexual relationships with men. No one doubted that she would marry someday. Her theme song announced, "You're gonna make it after all." It wasn't clear what that "after all" referred to, but we could relate.

To our surprise, another aspect of the counterculture had infiltrated the medical school. Our dean of students, a psychiatrist, turned out to be a devotee of est, a spin-off of the human potential movement. Est, or Erhard Seminars Training, was the brainchild of Werner Erhard, either a genius or a charlatan, depending on your point of view. He charged $250 for a weekend of consciousness raising which involved submitting to his will. He locked people in rooms and deprived them of food and sleep. He verbally abused them. We women figured we could handle verbal abuse, but when we heard that he didn't allow people to go to the bathroom, we lost interest.

First year, the dean of students came before us with a student from our class and one from a class a few years ahead of us. They had all been through the training and extolled its benefits. Lorraine remembers Erhard himself coming to give us his pitch. I don't remember him. What we all remember is the distinct impression that the inmates were in charge of the loony bin. Even if est turned out to be the cosmic answer, we found it profoundly disturbing that a member of the faculty with power over our lives was promoting it. We were worried that if we didn't participate, it would be held against us. Even if we were curious about it, none of us had an extra $250 to spare.

No one pressured us to take est after the presentation. The fact that we worried about it is significant, though. We were an anxious bunch, all too familiar with fending off peer pressure on every conceivable front. The Vietnam War was winding down when we started medical school in 1973, but the U.S. did not pull out of South Vietnam until 1975. The big news, other than the energy crisis in 1973, was the Watergate scandal. All summer, the nation watched the Senate hearings on TV.

When my husband and I drove across the country that summer, from Boston to San Francisco, the disembodied testimony from the radio kept us alert across the Great Plains. Barbara Jordan, the black senator from Texas with the commanding voice, instantly became our hero. She had been the first and only black woman in the Texas State Senate, where a colleague had called her "that old nigamammy washerwoman." Yet here she was, a U.S. Senator, pronouncing the words "My faith in the Constitution is whole, it is complete, it is total." When President Nixon resigned the following year, it was as though a great crack had appeared in the monolith of the "establishment," a word we women used indiscriminately to describe the federal government and the medical school hierarchy.

On September 20, 1973, a few weeks after we started medical school, 29-year-old Billie Jean King, the reigning Wimbledon women's singles champion, defeated Bobbie Riggs, a fifty-five-year-old man who had been the Wimbledon men's singles champion in 1939, in a tennis match. In 2007, this outcome does not seem surprising. We do not expect a man thirty years past his prime to be able to beat a woman who is an elite athlete, just because she is a woman. But at the time, this match was billed as "The Battle of the Sexes" and Riggs was a five-to-two favorite in Las Vegas. People didn't know what to think of a woman athlete or how to predict her performance. As Billie Jean King said, "In the'70s, we had to make it acceptable for people to accept girls and women as athletes. We had to make it OK for them to be active. Those were much scarier times for females in sports."

Any of us could make the same comment, substituting the word "doctors" for "athletes" and "medicine" for "sports." Like Billie Jean King, we understood that our presence in medical school was a political statement. King's use of the word "scarier" rings emotionally true. At the same time, we were buoyed by the achievements of the women we admired, like King, and Barbara Jordan, and Mary Tyler Moore. We were going to be part of a new world order, where people like Nixon wouldn't be president, and we all stood equal under the law. As we entered medical school, we imagined that the social and political changes we saw around us were a gathering wave.

Only in retrospect did we understand that the wave of social change crested and started to recede while we studied in the ivory towers. The year we entered medical school, minority admissions to UCSF peaked. It was also the year that Alan Bakke, a 32-year-old white man, applied to medical school at the University of California at Davis and was denied admission. He argued that he was more qualified than minority students who were admitted under different rules. In 1978, the Supreme Court of the United States agreed that he had been wrongfully denied admission. The five-to-four decision did not outlaw all consideration of race in admissions, since "diversity" was cited as a permissible goal in the process, but the ruling had a chilling effect on minority admissions at the University of California. By the time the decision was handed down, the impetus to achieve minority enrollment proportional to the population was spent, and minority students felt less welcome at the University.

The arc of the women's movement also peaked and started to decline while we were in training, although the number of women studying medicine continued to rise. In the early 1970s, feminist groups were busy lobbying for ratification of the Equal Rights Amendment to the constitution. The amendment stated, "Equality of rights under the law shall not be denied or abridged by the United States or by any State on account of sex." Thirty-eight states needed to ratify the amendment for it to become law. By 1977, thirty-five states had signed on, but there the movement stalled. The amendment died in 1982, still ratified by only 35 states. The opposition saw the amendment as a threat to the traditional family and as an assertion of federal power.

I was in Alaska on vacation in 1981 when I heard that the American Medical Association had come out against the ERA. The amendment was already in its death throes. I felt utterly betrayed by "my" professional organization. "Why did they have to take a public position at all?" I sputtered to my husband, while we stood in line at a salmon barbecue for tourists. A woman came up to me and said, "I overheard your conversation. You must be a doctor, too." It turned out that she was from Oakland, and she and I are still friends, linked by our femaleness in the profession.

When Patty Hearst was abducted from her house in 1974, we women thought it was another sign of a changing political order. Two months later she helped rob a bank near our campus. We were horrified, but riveted. Anything seemed possible in those days. In fact, the members of the Symbionese Liberation Army acted out a short-lived parody of a revolutionary movement and were forgotten as soon as their names left the headlines.

We girls stayed on in San Francisco for our residencies after medical school, so it is easy for us to pinpoint the day we knew that the liberal tide had ebbed. It was November 27, 1978, the day Dan White, a conservative city supervisor killed Harvey Milk, his colleague on the Board of Supervisors and the liberal mayor, George Moscone. Harvey Milk, our first openly gay supervisor, had championed the disenfranchised of every sexual persuasion. The tragedy was like a bad movie script, the literal revenge of the straight white man threatened by change.

Lorraine claims that when we were first-year students, I looked around the lecture room at our diverse class and said, "This medicine business can't be as good as they claim if they are letting all of us in." I don't remember saying it, but I could have. My father, the politician, was as cynical as they come, yet his answer, when asked how he was doing, was always, "Still struggling." The five of us are still struggling with our profession, in our own ways. We feel tremendously lucky to be witnesses to the genomic revolution and proud to be able to offer our patients the miracle technologies developed in our lifetimes. We love the science and the toys. We chose a wonderful trade. We feel we kept our part of the bargain, we gained the tools to serve society.

While we were in training, the political will of the country shifted in a way we never anticipated. As the income gap between the rich and the poor widened, health care became more of a privilege and less of a right. Judith and I became gatekeepers rationing care. Karen faced a managed care market that devalued the therapy she was trained to provide, in favor of best-selling drugs. Ruth, who loves to think through a clinical puzzle, faces an assembly line of ten colonoscopies each day. Lorraine found herself arguing against abandoning current patients when some of her colleagues wanted to dump managed care contracts. In our clinical practices, we careen between two poles of emotion, exasperation with the wild expectations of the affluent who are well and frustration with the lack of resources for those who are truly ill but poor.

We did not allow ourselves to think about words like exasperation and frustration as medical students in the seventies. Our political orientation, largely tacit, helped us survive our training. It did not enhance our job satisfaction once we faced the realities of our lives in practice. Looking back, we are bemused by our youthful idealism. But proud, too.

3. Revelations of the Third Year

"It might be true that the only way to establish yourself was to take the risk of making mistakes, but if the mistakes were the only things that were noticed, then all you proved was that you couldn't do it." (Carol Chetkovich, *Real Heat: Gender and Race in the Urban Fire Service*, 1997)

Judith recalls that on the first Monday of her medicine rotation, she and the other third-year student, also a woman, came prepared to present the patients they had admitted over the weekend. Attending rounds took place either in the small room behind the nurses' station, or in the solarium, a bright room lined with windows, intended for family visits. The attending physician was a faculty member overseeing the ward team: one resident and two interns. Each intern supervised a third-and a fourth-year student. The team stayed in the hospital overnight every third night. (The medicine clerkship was one of the most important, and the longest, at eight weeks. Surgery was also eight weeks, pediatrics and ob-gyn six weeks, neurology and psychiatry four.) A student presentation is an oral quiz: Judith was prepared to recite the patient's history and physical and discuss the patient's disease.

To her surprise, the attending didn't question Judith about her patient's case, but questioned the other student. Then he directed questions about the other woman's case to Judith. The two women struggled to come up with answers, but they didn't have an adequate fund of knowledge to discuss clinical problems off the cuff. Although this was normal for their stage of learning, they felt humiliated in front of the team. Judith and the other woman student quickly realized that if they shared their cases on Sunday evenings over the phone, they could both be better prepared on Monday. They used Sunday night to study the diseases of the other person's patients. Judith says she had qualms about this collusion, which they never revealed to the attending, but she saw no point in making herself vulnerable when she could avoid it. We women understood that it was considered bad form to work together, but it took us years to understand why.

Even if we had been able to formulate questions about the process, there was no one to ask. There was no time for reflection or discussion at all. In comparison, third-year students at UCSF now have a two-day intersession every few months, to talk over their clinical experiences, as well as "stress rounds" each week on the more intense clerkships like medicine. On "stress rounds" students can talk about deaths, mistakes, difficult patient encounters. When we faced disturbing experiences, we faced them alone. Given our idealism and naivete, we were continually surprised.

On my medicine rotation, my resident took me aside to prepare me for a presentation in front of a professor from another university (a visiting fireman, in medical jargon). This was quite an honor, for a third-year student to be chosen to speak for the team.

"Tell him the patient had 'rusty sputum,'" he said. Rusty, or blood-tinged, sputum helped distinguish pneumococcal pneumonia from other pneumonias.

"But he didn't," I protested. "I asked specifically. His sputum was yellow."

The resident looked at me as though I were addled.

"You have to say he had rusty sputum so that the attending can figure out the diagnosis easily. Your job is to make the attending look good."

This was my job? Not to accurately report the history and physical? I didn't want to believe it. But I complied. Another time the same resident told me, "It is important to work, but more important to be seen working." I will always be grateful to him for stating explicitly what other people assumed I knew. Lorraine feels the same way about a resident she had in her fourth year who took her aside and told her to practice her presentations in front of a mirror. She had looked upon the presentations as means of conveying information, not as performances.

Lorraine watched a neurology resident make up a history for a patient, for the benefit of another visiting fireman. The resident was so confident of the strength of the medical hierarchy that he didn't even ask Lorraine's cooperation in his falsehood. He launched into his fabricated history, knowing that the rest of the team would stay silent. Lorraine was shocked, but she didn't speak up. This was how the game was played.

Lorraine recognized the code we lived under when she read *The Right Stuff* by Tom Wolfe. She claims there was even a pseudo-Southern wisecracking style that male doctors affected. Military movies like *Top Gun* and *Men of Honor* helped me. In the military, guys in training have no recourse. They have to prove themselves alone, without any help from their friends. This was such a strange idea to us girls, that we weren't supposed to help anyone, that at first we didn't get it.

Nor did it occur to us that making our fellow students look bad was one way to get ahead.

In 1975, we women struggled in a system that didn't make sense to us. The British authors of the book *Athena Unbound*, who studied how women cope with science education twenty years later, think that the problems we faced are still relevant. "Most faculty members in science and engineering departments treat young women the same way as they treat young men. But this seeming equality differentiates against women in asking them to perform in ways that are contrary to their socialization. By 'challenging' everyone in the class to 'prove' themselves in the face of harsh teaching methods, rapid curriculum pace and a rigid assessment system, academic staff send a meaningless message to the female minority."

Judith's resident imitated the attending, putting Judith on the spot with obscure questions during ward rounds. If the patient mentioned that he had a headache, her resident might ask her to recite the different kinds of brain tumors and how often they occurred in a man this age. This process was called "pimping" a student (male or female). Although it was also called teaching, for us it was hard to see how asking questions that we couldn't possibly answer advanced our knowledge. After a week, Judith appealed to her (male) intern for protection and help. Fortunately, he was able to coach her on the kind of trivia the resident was likely to dredge up and to deflect some of the resident's attention by speaking up with answers himself when he knew them. Possibly because of her previous work life, Judith had a thick skin. She didn't take it all personally, and if she didn't know the answers, she didn't dwell on it. She chose internal medicine as a career, despite her mixed introduction to the field.

The third year of medical school was an important year because it was the foundation of our lives as clinicians. (So important, that the girls insisted that I write about it, even though I was reluctant to revisit territory I had covered in my first book.) On a practical level, the third year was our first opportunity to work with patients, our chance to rotate among the medical specialties. It was also a critical year in terms of forming our image of a doctor. As fledgling physicians, we were looking for someone to follow, to imprint. Unlike the men, who were stepping into a role familiar from life and from its reflections in books and on TV, to a great extent we had to imagine ourselves doctors.

We were anxious to display our "people skills," caring, and compassion. We felt scared as we stepped onto the wards, but our conceit was that here we would shine. Later we learned that some of our more savvy classmates had already begun to make steps toward residencies like dermatology and ophthalmology, which required earlier applications than other fields, but at the time, we were confident we were right on track. We had two years of classroom work and the first part of the national boards under our belt, like a nutritious breakfast before a grueling day.

None of us had settled on a specialty, although we had leanings. All of us would have said that we were interested in primary care. Women and blacks were supposed to be interested in primary care. Ruth also had her eye on an academic career. The more our group studied for the board exam, the more we looked forward to the people work. Our entire psychological focus was on the patients. In our fantasies, we imagined ourselves and the patients in a kind of splendid isolation. We didn't think much about other students or nurses or residents or attending physicians. Predictably, those were the people who tripped us up.

There were three teaching hospitals: the university hospital; the county hospital, San Francisco General; and the Veteran's Administration hospital. At the university hospital, a standard glass and high-rise structure, there were fewer patients and many had rare diseases. On the cancer ward and the endocrine specialty ward, patients were enrolled in clinical experiments. The hospital was located on Parnassus Heights, the ivory tower.

At the county hospital, there were many patients, mostly poor. The adults abused themselves with drugs and alcohol, and the children were often neglected. On the plus side, there was an exciting mix of ethnicities, and because the staff needed extra hands, even a medical student was welcome. The facility was scattered in several historic brick buildings, separated by gardens. There was an old TB unit, a locked psychiatric unit, and a locked jail ward for county inmates. The ancient wards did not have individual rooms. Instead, there were enormous spaces with beds lined up side by side. Old war movies often have scenes in hospitals organized the same way, with Florence Nightingales ministering to the injured troops. Just walking down the main aisle of the male ward, drawing the attention of dozens of bored patients on either side, was a daunting prospect for a 23-year-old woman.

The Veterans hospital was in-between. There were more patients than at the university and more staff than at the county. The building was a standard issue federal hulk overlooking the ocean, with old-fashioned touches like marble stalls in some of the ladies rooms. Emergency room and clinic patients shared a huge outpatient waiting room. We called it purgatory, because all the patients wanted to get into the hospital. V.A. patients, overwhelmingly men, had the common diseases of affluence: diabetes, heart attacks, gout. Most of them had chronic lung disease, too, from smoking. Cigarettes were part of rations in World War II and cheap in Vietnam. Everyone who rotated to the V.A. heard the apocryphal story about the German general who "recently toured a V.A. hospital." He looked around at the chronically ill vets and shook his head. "How did we lose the war!"

The attendings were mostly researchers who were required to spend one or two months on the wards, an obligation many of them viewed as just above committee work. There was a hematologist who acted as though he had an experiment boiling on a Bunsen burner, he zoomed through rounds so fast. On the other hand, some of the most eminent researchers were wonderful teachers, who took the opportunity to catch up on developments outside their field.

One prominent rheumatologist used to nibble like a rabbit at the corner of a sheet of paper while he listened to a presentation. His attention was so profound it was like a trance. There was a world-renowned Indian cardiologist whose kindness was legendary. The story goes that on morning rounds he once asked a bleary-eyed intern what side of the body the heart was on, and the muddled intern said, "The right side." The cardiologist answered crisply, in his British accent, "Very good, doctor. True, sometimes the heart is on the right. But more commonly, and in this patient, it is on the left." We felt lucky when we encountered one of these great teachers, and deprived when we did not. Today more physicians are hired mainly to teach, on clinical tracks separate from the research tracks.

We tried to do most of our rotations at the V.A. or the county, to gain the most experience. The locations were assigned by lottery. Lorraine remembers that when she received her last choice for medicine, the private service at the university hospital, where the attendings didn't allow students to do much, a wave of hopelessness passed over her. I felt fortunate to land internal medicine at the county. I had a woman intern both months, another stroke of luck, which probably directed me toward internal medicine as much as the intellectual content of the specialty did.

We girls tried to keep meeting every few weeks, although it was difficult with our various night call schedules. It was obvious at our first clerkship meeting that Ruth, our star student during the first two years, was not doing well on medicine at the V.A. The nurses and medical team were difficult. Ruth's team expected her to know how to start IVs and to perform spinal taps. Since it was her first third-year rotation, she had not yet learned how to do these procedures.

The intern wanted Ruth to be able to start an IV by herself, because he was so busy. Afraid to bother him, she thought maybe another student or a nurse could help her. But most of the students were no more skilled than she was, and the nurses didn't want to deal with teaching students, especially not women students.

It was the intern's job to supervise her, and he did when Ruth failed and returned to ask his help, but he was impatient.

"How could they expect us to know how to do things no one had taught us?" Lorraine demanded when Ruth reminded us of those days recently. "And why did we think it was our fault?" Ruth added. We agreed that we would know how to handle such a situation today. We would say right away, "I'd love to learn how to start an IV, but you'll have to teach me." Ruth did not have the nerve to be honest about her skills in those days, partly because, as a woman, she was afraid of appearing timid. None of us had been taught to start an IV, but somehow we all felt that the men knew how to bluff their way through better.

We women were also reluctant to practice on patients without any guidance. To this day, the motto that summed up how procedures were taught, "See one, do one, teach one" makes me uneasy. We knew, even at the time, that this was a woman thing. Most of the men seemed to feel entitled to do anything to a patient, because they were medical students. It was a sign of weakness to ask how to do a procedure or to admit not knowing a fact. "Never say 'I don't know,'" a neurosurgeon screamed at a fellow (male) student on rounds one day. When I say screamed, I mean screamed, so loud that everyone in the hall, nurses, patients, and other doctors turned around to stare. Every time I see a doctor get into trouble because he isn't honest with himself about his limitations and refuses to ask for help, I think of that student.

There was also a more subtle psychological reason to explain why we initially found procedures difficult. Unlike the men, who only had to worry about technical mastery and internal qualms, we had to convince the patients, as well as ourselves, that we could assume this doctor role. There is some prejudice against "rookie" doctors of either sex. But in those days there was considerably more resistance to the idea of a woman rookie. We were frequently told, "You don't look like a doctor." We understood that this might have been intended as a compliment, as in "You're too attractive to be a doctor," but it didn't feel like a compliment.

Medicine was also my first third-year rotation, but neither of my women interns expected me to be able to do anything useful at the beginning. I felt it was okay to try and fail and try again. One patient on my ward required an IV started every day, because the amphotericin (amphoterrible, we called it, because of its side effects) needed to fight an infection in his knee destroyed the vein after one dose. He was an old black farmer from the Central Valley, sent up to the Big City because his infection was rare. He knew I was the least experienced person on the team, but he encouraged me to keep poking. He was proud of me for being a black woman medical student, and did his best to help me. (Today, the radiologists would use ultrasound to locate a large vein and place a more permanent line that would last the duration of the therapy.)

When Ruth described her unhappiness, I thought of this patient with the infected knee. He tooled around in a wooden wheelchair as old as he was, the bad leg elevated. He called the chair his "Cadillac." I looked forward to his smile, because even on my medicine rotation, with pleasant people, I felt stressed out most of the time. I told Ruth so. She turned to me and asked, "But do you cry every day?" No, I didn't. That came later. Fortunately, Ruth met her future husband, David, who was a medical resident, on her medicine rotation. He was older, back in training after a stint in the military. (Starting in the 1950s, all male doctors were subject to a "doctor draft," two years of mandatory service in the Army, Navy, Air Force, or Public Health Service. This ended after the Vietnam War.) David's experience gave him a broader perspective. He could tell Ruth that whether or not she could start an IV was not a measure of her worth as a physician. We were relieved when she came to the next meeting in better spirits.

Ruth and David literally met over a patient. They were holding down the arms of a man while a pulmonary doctor looked into his lungs through a tube. (Patients are sedated for the procedure, but still conscious and sometimes combative in their confusion.) Ruth asked David later what first attracted him to her.

"You seemed very professional for a third-year student," he answered.

"Wrong!" she declared, laughing. She had hoped he would comment on something a little more personal.

But whatever the attraction, it was mutual. Ruth moved in with him after the second date. "Are you kidding?" she asked, when we expressed surprise at how fast she had mobilized. "I was living in an apartment with no heat" (there was some heat, Karen maintains), "I didn't have the twelve dollars to pay my electric bill, my parents had just separated and couldn't help me financially, and I don't cook. Here was a man who loved me as a doctor, had his own house with central heating, paid my electric bill, and fixed me dinner every night. It was a no-brainer." Plus he was Jewish, she didn't need to add. "A man who loved me as a doctor" has resonance for all of us. We all wanted partners to love us as doctors, not in spite of the fact that we were doctors.

Ruth did not tell us during third year that the attending physician on her first rotation propositioned her. He sent her a note that said, "I like to look at your breasts" and asked for a date. She did not know how to deal with this advance. "I felt ashamed and dirty," she said last year when she finally revealed the secret. "I thought it was my fault." She declined his offer as politely as she could, because she was concerned about her grade. Fortunately, he did not retaliate against her. Needless to say, she didn't tell anyone in authority about the attending's behavior. She did not have the words to speak: "sexual harassment" was a concept yet to emerge.

The attending physicians were grown-ups, not peers. There were women who dated them, but it was assumed that these were women trying to advance their careers on the casting couch, not women pursuing a relationship of equals. The hierarchy in medicine was rigid. One of the scariest aspects of our clinical training was that there seemed to be no guideposts, that the whims of attending physicians determined our fates. We used to laugh at the idea that women couldn't be surgeons by commenting, "They don't operate with their penises do they?"

In a sense, many men did operate with their penises in those days, because their sexuality was at play in any interaction with a woman. A (male) resident once warned me that a man always had to consider whether he would sleep with a woman before he could work with her. Today, when women comment on men's butts on prime-time TV and Meredith Grey sets the standard for the professional woman, young women may feel free to express their sexuality overtly in the workplace. We did not.

The long hours, the nights, the intensity of the work led to a sexually charged atmosphere. In addition, a whole class of women, the nurses, were used to owning the male doctors at work. The nurses were the traditional wives, who took orders from the doctors. As medical students, we challenged the time-honored balance of power between the sexes. Our existence threatened the nurses, and their marriage prospects, and with few exceptions, they made our lives more difficult. Certainly they responded faster when an attractive guy gave the order. In the county emergency room, I heard a nurse refer to a patient who was a prostitute as a "cunt." It was the first time I had heard that word from a woman's mouth. It offended every bone in my body, feminist, female, doctor, but speaking up to a veteran nurse was as impossible as speaking up to an attending doctor.

The older generation of women doctors often chose to be asexual, to fit in with the boys. We weren't aiming for that level of self-denial but we didn't want to jeopardize our professional stance either. On rounds, especially in the Intensive Care Units, where the best and brightest of the nurses gravitated, I resented waiting for the flirting between the nurses and my colleagues to subside so that we could consider the patients. Frequently it took several minutes for the team to gather at the nursing station in the ICU. Everyone with a beeper triaged problems over the phone while waiting. During that time, a nurse might comment that a male resident looked tired, and massage his shoulders. Or she would offer to call the lab for him, a favor never extended to women.

Was it a "hostile environment" as legally defined? No one was trying to make the women medical students feel uncomfortable (most of the time). Just another opportunity to feel awkward. Lorraine notes how much emotional energy we were forced to expend negotiating this terrain. I met a woman recently who was one of those ICU nurses, engaged at the time to a man in our class. She said she didn't think much about the women medical students. She was secure in her role and had a great time with the men. She was surprised that we women medical students felt left out.

It was difficult to move from clerkship to clerkship, facing forced intimacy with another group of strangers for a month or two. It was like starting a new job eight times in one year. Once we got past "Where are you from?", making small talk on the first day was excruciating. Most men could fall back on sports talk, but none of the five of us could. Meeting new colleagues was especially exasperating for me, because people often mistook me for another swarthy ethnicity (Latina, Arab?) rather than a light-skinned African-American. When I set one intern straight, she exclaimed, "That's like having to announce your gender!" No, but it wasn't fun either.

Most black people recognized me. Those who didn't would ask me if I were from New Orleans. New Orleans, the home of the Creole, is well known as a place of racial mixing. I would say, "No, but my people are from Savannah." They understood that a woman one generation out of the South who looked like me was black.

Karen had a wonderful time on psychiatry, working with a head nurse who shared her interests and took her in hand. It was the one rotation where she felt she fit in as a woman. Some of the residents were women, and none of them, even the men, were the kind of workaholics who dominated the other services. She recognized that psychiatry was not particularly well respected at UCSF and arranged to do a fourth-year psychiatry rotation at Beth Israel in Boston, which gave her a better view of the field.

Karen also managed to keep more of an outside life going than the rest of us did. Until Ruth left to live with David, she and Karen had shared an apartment, which Karen remembers with fondness. She plays the flute, and a man next door was a friend of Jean-Pierre Rampal, the world-renowned flautist. Rampal came to the apartment and played, a moment which was a highlight of Karen's life. Somehow, Karen even managed to take flute lessons those crazy years. She remembers practicing in the on-call room. It was a way to transport herself from the hospital.

Karen also remembers third year as the time she thought seriously about quitting school. She was already clear that she didn't want medicine to be her whole world. She remembers her medical resident sending the students out to get Mexican food. The county hospital is located in the Mission district, the Latino neighborhood in San Francisco. It felt like such a treat, to escape the hospital for a few minutes, to smell toasted chilies and cilantro instead of rubbing alcohol and shit. It made the rest of the clerkship bearable.

Overall, Karen probably has the least unhappy memories of the year, but she was also most impressed with the capriciousness of the clerkship system. After two years of moving as a huge group, lecture to lab, eight to five, all the students, men and women, had to maneuver almost alone. While there may have been a standard curriculum, it was up to the individual physicians whether they bothered to teach it. Many of them didn't seem to care if the students, particularly the women, learned anything or not. We expected that our apprenticeship would be arduous, but the indifference took us by surprise. Although we faced board exams again at the end of fourth year, when we would have to demonstrate broad clinical knowledge, luck determined whether a service was busy, so that we were exposed to many patients and diseases, and whether we had a resident who was interested in teaching. Today there are more formal classroom sessions, even when students are on the wards, and the students evaluate the residents as well as vice versa. Formal mentoring systems are also common.

When Lorraine rotated through pediatrics at the County, she worked with a thoughtful chief resident, two women residents, and an intern who all ultimately ended up in pediatric dermatology, as she did. One of the women had taken time off to have a child and was now sharing a residency. That would be unremarkable now, but then it was groundbreaking. It was no accident that this innovation occurred in the pediatrics department. In 1970, when only 8 percent of doctors were women, pediatrics already had 20 percent women, compared to 6 percent in internal medicine. The research suggests that when a minority reaches 15 percent of the population, this "critical mass" is adequate to influence the majority culture. The culture of pediatrics accommodated women earlier, so it was less foreign to us. "They seemed like normal people," Lorraine remembers. This may seem an odd way to describe a bright group who are all professors today, but we understood what she meant. These were people who were not ashamed to admit to a life outside of medicine. They did not hide behind arrogance or pretend they knew everything. "I felt like I could be myself around them," she adds.

Pediatrics was the highlight of Lorraine's year, the place where she felt at home. As she had feared, her medicine clerkship was disappointing. Many of the private patients barely tolerated the interns and residents, and wanted as little to do with students as possible. She hated the way internists used knowledge as a weapon, citing journal articles in an endless game of one-upmanship. To make matters worse, her resident kept asking her out. She ultimately did date him briefly ("he was nice enough"), but she wasn't attracted to him.

This interaction would be defined today as sexual harassment. It bothered Lorraine at the time, but with our long days and night call, it was difficult to meet men outside of medicine. We had also noticed that in general, the men outside of medicine were much less supportive of the women in medicine than vice versa. Wives might complain, but they respected their husbands' passion and looked forward to better days. Husbands considered themselves supportive when they asserted that the process was idiotic and encouraged their wives to quit. Bob, Judith's husband, was one of the more tolerant ones. As a young lawyer in a big firm, he was putting in long hours in order to make partner, so he didn't have time to hang out either.

We all felt vulnerable in those first days on the wards. Karen never lacked for dates, but she felt she couldn't make a commitment to someone during the craziness of the wards. Even in the first two years of medical school, when she was dating guys in the class, her relationships tended to end around exam time, because she was too stressed to deal with men then. When Karen and Lorraine lived together, later, Lorraine was jealous of all the men buzzing around Karen. But Karen remembers breaking off relationships because she anticipated that guys would expect her to give up her professional goals, even if it hadn't come up yet. She ran across some of the "stereotypical self-centered MD" types, too. Third year, Karen started therapy, which she credits with helping her figure out how much stress was impacting her personal life.

Lorraine, like Ruth, plunged into a relationship with a medical resident within a few weeks of starting her clerkships. She met him in the emergency room, where we had all noticed him. He was Japanese-American, with hair below his shoulders and a quiet confidence, half Zen monk, half cowboy. At first she was flattered to attract his attention, but it quickly became clear that she was one of several women he was seeing. His apartment was just a few blocks from the hospital, and he didn't have a phone, partly, she suspected, so his women couldn't reach him. I remember her describing the "incredible" texture of his skin to me. I should have known then that she would end up in dermatology.

Although "the sex was like a drug," she broke it off after a few months because she felt like a groupie. Yet she followed his progress. Near the end of his residency, burnt out from training, he decided to join a medical mission to Central

America. When he died in a plane crash in Guatemala, Lorraine was devastated. "I felt like anyone I got close to, first my parents and now this boyfriend, was marked for death." Years later, investigation revealed that the military shot down the plane because one of the passengers was an activist priest. Lorraine's personal loss was a political death.

Past the newlywed stage, Judith and I struggled to maintain emotional contact with our husbands. My husband Miles and I took medicine together at the county hospital. We didn't see each other, except in passing, since we were on different teams. After our first night on call, Miles took our only car and drove home. He had completely forgotten me. Judith remembers trying to socialize with a couple she and Bob had met on vacation. They spent a day mostly naked with several other couples learning massage, not that unusual an activity for a young couple in the seventies, but worlds away from medicine and corporate law. Too far, they decided. She and Bob regretted the time they had wasted that day.

Surgery was the bastion of sexism in clinical medicine, and we all knew it beforehand. Our experiences ranged from neutral to awful. At that time at UCSF, third-year students worked up and presented patients and attended lectures, but did not see the inside of an operating room. This was a contrast to the hands-on experience of the other clerkships and generated some grumbling. On the other hand, the bookwork was familiar territory, with reliable feedback.

In the first few weeks of the eight-week clerkship, the lowest grade I received on my written work was a B. So when the chief of surgery, not the attending physician assigned to me, called my assigned partner and me in for a chat, I was puzzled. (I had already had "a little chat" with my own attending, who was disappointed that I didn't practice any high risk sports. Why didn't I ski? I pointed out that Chicago and Washington, D.C., where I had been raised, were far from ski resorts and that lift tickets were expensive. I could tell that wasn't the right answer.)

My partner, a guy I didn't know well before the clerkship, was a handsome man with a good sense of humor. He had the reputation of a solid student. Which was lucky, since we had to spend almost every working hour of those eight weeks together. We walked into the chief's office and waited until he asked us to sit down. He was a small man, sitting across from us at a desk stacked with papers and journals. He came straight to the point.

"The two of you have a bad attitude. If you don't straighten up, you're going to flunk this course." We knew what that meant: we'd have to take it over. It was required.

"Any questions?" No. We already understood that questions would get us in more trouble. "Never complain, never explain." We didn't dare look at each other until he had dismissed us and we were outside.

"The guy's psychotic!" my partner exclaimed when we were out of earshot.

I tried to believe him, but I couldn't shake off the chief's words. How could he be psychotic? He was the chief of the department. I must secretly be a bad student.

To this day I have no idea what triggered the surgeon's outburst. I had never flunked a course in my life, and there was no objective indication that I was flunking this one. My reaction was so stereotypically female that I am embarrassed to write about it. My partner had enough self-confidence to dismiss the chief's assessment. I didn't. We were the pre-Title IX girls. Title IX, the federal legislation that guaranteed "equal opportunity" for girls in sports, was passed in 1972. We had no experience of team sports or the military or other settings where we could have learned to shrug off abuse. On the contrary. We had always been praised. Such good students. Even in science. Remarkable for girls.

Quarter break, a week off, fell between my two months of surgery. Miles and I went camping with friends from school. Driving back over the Bay Bridge, I burst into tears. I told him I couldn't return to school, that I wasn't strong enough to be a doctor. Even before I met the chief of surgery, I had to talk myself out of my anxiety each day to go to work. (Lorraine says, "I'm just as anxious as other women. I just don't let it stop me.") Miles calmed me down. I returned, and I finished the surgery rotation, taking my cue from my partner, who didn't talk about what had happened, but hunkered down in the library. We studied late every night because it seemed that in order not to "flunk" we would have to pull A's. (Yes, the clerkship was technically pass/fail, but the surgeons graded each piece of written work and each presentation.) At home, I had started crying every day.

Third year was not the first time I had faced depression, although it was the first time I could name it. Now I have lived long enough to know that crises in my life invite depression to visit. Darkness is my old friend. Even then, I sought help, but the woman therapist at student health dismissed me by saying, "You're a black woman in medical school; what did you expect?" She told me that I didn't need to make a second appointment. Years later, another therapist asked me if I felt angry about how I'd been treated. I didn't have the perspective to be angry. I knew that medical school was supposed to be hard, so I assumed that the first therapist was telling me that my suffering was within normal limits.

After my experience at student health, I didn't speak to a therapist again until after the birth of my second child, almost ten years later. Karen began therapy third year and continued through her residency. Ruth and Lorraine started as residents, coincidentally with the same therapist. (They didn't speak of it at the time; I figured it out after interviewing both of them.) Judith was the only one of us who didn't seek professional help, because she didn't think exploring her mind would improve her situation. She has a point. We have all worked hard to determine which problems arise from our personalities and which from the sociological facts of our lives. One of our professors, now a professor emeritus, pointed out that many of the early women doctors came from affluent families, so at least they had the entitlement of the rich. We had no money behind us, little family support (my father asked, "Why do you want to deal with the shit of the world?"), and (some) teachers and classmates told us that we didn't belong in medical school. Most human beings would be anxious under similar conditions.

Were we tougher by the end of the third year? You betcha. Even when we were most conflicted and miserable, we soldiered on. Junior (third year) surgery had been such a negative experience that three of us did senior surgery (also required) on the Kidney Transplant Unit, where there was both a medical and a surgical attending physician. We knew we wouldn't learn much surgery since students didn't go to the operating room on that rotation, but it was a way of decreasing the power of the surgeons to destroy us. Later, as a dermatologist, Lorraine learned that she enjoyed doing minor procedures such as skin biopsies, and today much of her work involves lasers. She regrets her minimal surgery training. But, as she puts it, "The part of myself who liked surgery was inaccessible because of the social situation."

This was the nightmare of third year. We girls had counted on being able to succeed through perseverance, even if the way was steep. One step after another. We didn't expect people to trip us. When they did, we ruminated over it, looking for meaning that wasn't there. A male friend who endured similar hazing on his surgery clerkship is amazed that we didn't know that men in power often "fuck with you because they can." Nothing personal.

Today, clinical instructors like myself are told to sandwich any criticism of a student between two statements of praise. It turns out that intimidation is not the most efficient way to teach critical thinking. Women of our generation have played an important role in changing the culture of medical education. As outsiders, we were shocked by the toll it took on students, men and women. At the same time, my women students have been raised on the playing field as well as in the classroom, so they are better prepared.

We didn't trust ourselves, we were wary of physicians above us in the hierarchy, and we couldn't count on the nurses. Was this different from how the men felt? It is hard to know, since we were afraid to reveal our true feelings in front of our male classmates. For the men in our class, the choice of a medical career was a conservative one, often following in their fathers' footsteps. If we women had followed the parallel path outlined for our gender, we would have been stay-at-home moms in the suburbs. Miles certainly had a better experience. In retrospect, he was able to separate his own experience from the group in a way that was very helpful. If an attending yelled at another student, my husband's reaction was, "Whew, dodged a bullet there." Then he moved on. Too often, I cringed in empathy.

My husband and I did few rotations together, but pediatrics was one of them. My evaluation said that I wasn't assertive enough. Miles didn't say anything at all in the sessions with the chief, but a six-foot-three black man is always assertive. This was one of many times that I would suffer in comparison to my husband. All medical students are competitive. We had to be competitive to get in. And the system fostered competition rather than dampening it. Most of the time, I didn't feel competitive with my husband or the girls: on the contrary, I took pleasure in their success.

I sometimes resented the attention Miles received, however. He seemed to lead a charmed life. Handsome, preppy, and personable, he made white people feel comfortable. They could point to him as the example and ignore the rest of the black students. I overheard grumbling from some of those students behind his back, because people didn't always know that we were married. (Of course, with my coloring, many people didn't think I was black, anyway.) One chief of service used to put his arm around Miles and present him as a Harvard football player.

Miles graduated from Harvard, but he did not play football there. He was proud that his admission to Harvard was based on brains and not brawn. He tried to tell the attending (a Harvard alumnus himself) that he hadn't played football, but the attending clung to the stereotype of the black Ivy athlete. One day when the attending started on about Harvard football again, and Miles was trying to speak up, I hissed out of earshot of the attending, "Oh, shut up and let him say so. You'll never convince him otherwise." He took my advice.

Another time, an intern who had worked with my husband and also with me, watched an attending beam at Miles as he presented a case. Nods and smiles and words of encouragement. "Must be hard for you," he whispered. It was. Without the reality check of my conversations with the girls, I would have thought I was crazy. The sociologist Carol Chetkovich found that women had a harder time than black men as rookie firefighters. "Among men, race matters: the paths of some men are less sure than the paths of others, and experiences of racial suspicions and exclusions do emerge. But gender matters in a different, deeper and more consistent way." That was certainly my experience. My husband is a great guy and a great doctor, but inertia is probably the only reason we didn't break up third year. Apart from the competition, we were working so hard that we had no energy left for our relationship.

I recognized my husband's coping pattern in Melvin Konner's book *Becoming A Doctor*. Because he is an anthropologist, I expected Konner to comment on the experiences of students around him as he went through medical school, particularly possible outsiders like women. Yet his memoir is strictly personal. His third year was not happy, but he was already relatively well known in another profession, which made him considerably less vulnerable to ego erosion than the average student. And when push came to shove, he used his maleness to bond in a way that was impossible for us. Describing a conversation during a meal with his team, he wrote, "I took advantage of the lull. 'Yeah. He fucked her brains out and now she's on Flagg Seven.' This got one of the biggest laughs of the evening and secured me a place as a 'regular guy.'" We were not regular guys.

At the same time, we could not relate to the few women attending physicians of the older generation we encountered. They relished the compliment the women's movement had taught us to reject: "You think just like a man." Lorraine reminded us that the scuttlebutt on one woman surgeon was that she was so tough that she performed rectal exams without gloves. A tough, fast-talking New York cardiologist was mean to everyone. Students were scared to present to her. There was a brilliant, plain attending on medicine who always wore black, smoked, and never married or had children. I still admire her, but I admire her the way I would admire a scholarly nun.

Minority students had the Black Caucus behind them, but no similar movement supported women. Perhaps I could have benefited more from my minority credentials, but by the time we reached the wards, there was only one other black woman in the class. And I did not feel close to many of the black men. One classmate told a table of us at lunch that he'd decided to be a doctor when he'd realized that the life of a pimp was difficult to sustain. He was joking (all the men laughed) but I never ate lunch with him again. Another classmate once told me that my husband was the only man he had never heard make sexist comments, even in private. I thought, "That's my guy." Yet Miles hung around with some guys who made me squirm. It's different for men.

It was difficult for us women to wholeheartedly assume the doctor persona, the way the men did. Chetkovich, writing about the firefighters says, "Full identification with the traditional masculine identity was impossible, but a viable alternative wasn't all that clear." We imprinted where we could, but many days it was all we could manage to stay on track in the halls of distorting mirrors. We donned our doctor role for work and took it off, like support hose, when we came home. This was the birth of the "woman doctor." All of the women in our group eventually chose fields where women doctors now make up at least 20 percent of the work force, as opposed to surgery.

By the end of third year, medicine had changed us, although already Karen was actively resisting and I was questioning the constraints of the doctor identity. We all found internship and residency easier psychologically than medical school. The work was endless, but we knew how to work hard. We didn't have to curry favor for grades or sparkle on rounds. The glossy person who comes on like gangbusters does well on the short clerkship rotations. In residency, competence and consistency counted more than flash. Slowly, we regained the confidence that we had lost third year, and grew into a doctor identity that was temporarily very close to that of the men. Then we had to face the outside world, which wasn't ready for us either.

4. Seven Black Pantsuits and the Pill

"Look, I don't care if you *promise* me cancer in five years, I'm staying on the pill. At least I'll enjoy the five years I have left." (Housewife in the seventies. quoted by Lara V. Marks in *Sexual Chemistry: A History of the Contraceptive Pill*, 2001)

When Hillary Clinton won the Senate race in New York, she held a jubilant press conference. Quietly she described the beginning of the campaign, when victory seemed a long shot. Then, she smiled and gloated, "Seven black pantsuits later ..." The crowd interrupted with applause and shouts. She didn't have to add any more. The audience knew she meant, "Now, that I've won ..." Today the black pantsuit is the uniform of the active professional woman. It wasn't always so. When we were in medical school, our struggle to find a practical, professional way to dress mirrored our struggle to imagine ourselves doctors.

The issue of contraception was the hidden equivalent of our sartorial dilemma. We faced a minimum of seven years during which pregnancy would be highly undesirable. We had to choose between the early Pill, which made us sick and had no long-term track record, the IUD, which was just beginning to be prescribed for women who had not had children, and barrier methods, like the diaphragm and the condom, which were safe, but less reliable. From today's perspective it is easy to think, wear pants, take the pill. In those days neither choice was obvious.

Until the third year of medical school, we wore jeans, like the guys. Lorraine, Karen and I were graduates of the hippie fashion school. As a geology major in college, I had dressed for the outdoors. Lorraine lived in a commune in Seattle in between her college years. Karen followed the proud countercultural tradition of UC Berkeley. Judith and Ruth didn't aspire to be mountain men or hippies, but they were serious students who were used to grabbing what was easiest to wear, without a lot of fuss. A skirt with stockings and heels was always more work than jeans.

When they went on the wards, the men switched to dressier pants, mostly khakis. Wool suit pants were not practical in an environment where many patients spurted blood. Before AIDS, doctors didn't gown and glove except in the operating room. (We cared for many gay men with mysterious illnesses before the immune problem was defined. We were lucky to avoid HIV infection.) We women preferred to dress like the men, but for us, pants were not considered professional attire. Most of us had not been allowed to wear pants to school until college. Nice restaurants downtown still refused service to women in pants. A woman's suit was a jacket and a skirt, not pants.

Toward the end of second year, the women in the class started to worry about buying clothes to go on the wards. Lorraine and I found a consignment store where we could buy secondhand skirts cheaply. Going there was like taking a field trip to another world, a world where Junior League matrons changed clothes every season and sold them on commission. The irony of adapting castoffs from the world of leisure for our workaholic lifestyle was not lost on us. As we searched through the racks, we rejected the outfits that were too fashionable. We did not want to draw attention to ourselves. Fashion was outside our experience and our hope.

We were not the only professional women floundering in the clothing stores. In 1978, the book *Dress for Success* by John T. Malloy appeared, which codified the professional look for women. He favored suits with skirts, the best quality a woman could afford. These were worn with low-heeled pumps and stockings. His recommendations quickly became a uniform, to the point that stores no longer stocked daytime dresses. Our friends who worked in offices were relieved to adopt the look.

Malloy's suggestions didn't work for us. Only Karen, as a psychiatrist, sat most of the day, so she could have worn a skirt and heels if she wanted to. The rest of us were on our feet, up to thirty-six hours at a time. Nurses wore oxfords or tennis shoes for their eight-hour shifts. Oxfords with skirts looked dowdy, precisely the spinster doctor look we wanted to avoid. Tennis shoes were too casual. (Women rarely wore athletic shoes on the street. I remember buying my first pair of running shoes when Karen and I ran the Bay to Breakers race in 1975.) We compromised with flat-soled shoes like loafers that looked acceptable with skirts. These were not easy to find in a world where the low-heeled pump was the daytime shoe of choice.

Next came the problem of the suit jacket. As internists, Judith, Ruth, and I each wore a white coat. Lorraine, as a pediatrician, did not wear a white coat because it frightened the children. Karen could have worn a white coat if she wanted to, but didn't feel she needed it, either to establish authority or to protect her clothes. She also didn't need it to carry around a stethoscope, a reflex hammer, a vision-testing card, a second "code blue" beeper, and a notebook we called our "peripheral brain." In those days before Palm Pilots, we internists kept notebooks full of tiny scribblings of the most important formulas and tables we needed. Once a month we carried Tampax as well, since we were frequently far from our purses. We locked our purses in drawers on one ward, but we could find ourselves stuck in the emergency room or another ward for hours. We didn't need money, except for vending machines, when we were on call, because cafeteria meals were free. It was impossible to wear a suit jacket under the white coat: there wasn't enough arm room even if we could stand the heat.

The men didn't wear their suit jackets under their white coats either. They worked in shirts and ties, another piece of the uniform. The tie was disputed during our "years of ferment," but nearly everyone wore it at the university hospital, and nearly everyone didn't at the county hospital. Some of us felt that not wearing a tie at the county was a subtle sign of disrespect for the poor patients, but if so, the attending physicians who didn't enforce the tie rule there were complicit. We women had to make blouse decisions. Not too sheer, not too low, not too uptight. We couldn't afford silk, polyester looked tacky, and we didn't want to iron cotton. We wore modest blouses in cotton-poly blends until T-shirts and turtlenecks became acceptable under a jacket.

The pediatricians dressed more casually, because they were often stooping over or romping with children. Lorraine wore pants almost exclusively during her pediatric residency. When she metamorphosed into a dermatologist, she started wearing a white coat again and looking for dresses like the rest of us. We used to wear long, full skirts for mobility. There was no way to run for a Code Blue in a tight skirt. As interns in the Department of Medicine, Ruth and I were issued white A-line skirts that landed a little below the knee. Pants weren't offered to the women. We wore the skirts on days when we didn't have to spend the night. Unlike most women's skirts, they had pockets on which to hook a beeper.

At night, most of us wore scrubs we stole from the operating room. Our sleeping quarters were coed, so we wanted to stay covered. Some tiresome men insisted they had to sleep in the buff to emphasize their point that women didn't belong in the on-call room (or in medicine) but we simply averted our eyes. I never took off my bra, which worked only because if I had a chance to sleep I was so tired I collapsed. I had heard a story about a pediatric resident whose breasts could be seen swinging loose under her top when she was called to perform chest compressions for CPR in the middle of the night. Not me, babe.

Men watched what we wore. We women understood this and did our best to look presentable. Judith's waist-length straight hair, her signature then and now, was always pulled back or in a bun. So was Karen's hair. The rest of us had short or very short hair in wash-and-wear styles. Finding time for a haircut was a real challenge. Some women managed regular makeup, although our group was not consistently in their number. After all, our attendings were still teaching "the lipstick sign" (when a woman patient puts on her lipstick, she is ready to leave the hospital). I could never wear mascara, because a day rarely passed without a story sad enough to make me teary. We all had to keep our nails short for examining people. Imagine a rectal exam with nail extenders.

For years, I carefully alternated pants and skirts to avoid derogatory comments. ("Dyke" was a common insult, because we had to be "butch" to be in medical school.) Men insisted that I only wore pants anyway, proving again that we see what we want to see. One obnoxious resident told me that a particular intern was not a good doctor because she didn't shave her legs. In training, none of us dared ignore the issue of our looks, because it was clear that a brilliant man might be forgiven a sloppy appearance, but a brilliant woman would be passed over. And studies show that patients, especially older patients, especially black patients, prefer that their doctors dress more formally, wear a white coat.

My husband once received this comment on a positive medical school evaluation: "Well-groomed and arrives on time." By taking a shower and getting to class, he had exceeded this professor's expectations of a black student. As women, we were fighting similar stereotyping, trying to walk a line between flirty lightweight and dowdy brain. It was exhausting.

Once we went into practice, where men wore suits, we girls had to rethink the wardrobe question. We needed to look prosperous, not just presentable. Ruth and I couldn't hide in the white skirt uniform. Doing our time on planet hospital, we had lost touch with fashion. Judith and I took no time off and had babies within a year of finishing, so never had the luxury of time to go shopping for ourselves. I depended on L.L. Bean for cotton shells to wear under my white coat.

Lorraine went to have her "colors done," which was popular in those days. For a fee, a consultant determined which season (winter, spring, summer, fall) corresponded to your skin and hair tones and which shades of color would be most flattering. "Having my colors done was a way of acknowledging that you could use fashion to have an impact on how people perceived you. It appealed to me more than going to a fashion consultant who would dress me. I was afraid I would lose myself in the process."

It is still difficult, years later, to find dresses to wear under a white coat. Mallory's "Dress for Success" look dominates the stores, although there are as many pants suits today as suits with skirts. Dresses are relics for evening wear. When we first went into practice, only Karen felt she could wear "nice pants." Her reasoning: "Most of my patients were young women like myself." It took longer for the older generation to accept women in pants, but now that we are middle-aged ourselves, the issue has dissolved. Even Lorraine, who does the most public speaking, doesn't feel obligated to wear a skirt anymore.

Ruth shocked the rest of us at one of our discussions by announcing that she wears only operating-room scrubs at work, even in her consulting office when she is not doing procedures. "I was fed up with trying to be a doctor and a fashion model at the same time." She felt she was one of the best gastroenterologists around, and people would have to accept her without the froufrou. "And they have," she adds, triumphant.

The connection between clothing and power plays out in many ways. A few years ago, I practiced with a group of doctors at Summit Hospital in Oakland. We paid consultants to ask other members of the medical staff what they thought of us, because we wanted to generate more referral business. The group, founded by four women doctors, was predominately female.

The consultants presented their findings to our group. One of the major complaints was that the male medical staff had trouble recognizing us as doctors, despite our identification tags. We dressed too casually, they said, so they confused us with nurses or patients' families. I always wore a white coat, partly to establish my authority, partly to protect my clothes, but some of the women didn't. Those of us who had been in practice fifteen or twenty years knew that we would never look like doctors to men whose image of a doctor is a man. (When I was younger, I was amazed that my male colleagues never recognized me on the street, in casual clothes. And that some male doctors introduced themselves to me two and three times.) In a 1996 survey of fourth-year medical students, 3 percent of male students and 92 percent of female students reported that they had been mistaken for non-physicians.

"We could wear evening dresses and tiaras, to look more formal," a friend my age suggested bitterly at the meeting with the consultants. "That would distinguish us from the nurses." Instead we instituted a mandatory white coat rule. The white coats had our names embroidered on them, with the MD. The bottom line is that men will always "look like a doctor" even dressed for the golf course, and women still have to send clear visual clues to be recognized as doctors.

The question of clothing came to a head in third year when we started on the wards. The issue of birth control had arisen much earlier in our lives. The birth control pill was approved in 1960. Today people celebrate the 40th anniversary of the Pill as though it solved all possible contraceptive problems. Nothing could be further from the truth, especially for health-conscious women who wanted to keep childbearing options open. By the time we girls were in college, reports of serious side effects of the Pill were hitting the media. Again we were the in-between generation, coming of age after the drawbacks of the original pills were revealed and before studies proved the safety of the modern low-dose pill.

All of us tried the Pill at some point. The first pills on the market had 100-170 mcg of estrogen and 10 mg of progesterone, four or five times the amount of hormones in the pills today. They made me feel like throwing up, an unwelcome preview of morning sickness. Judith recalls, "They made me feel awful. Like I was dragging around, nauseated." Ruth remembers leg cramps. These were minor side effects, but at the same time most of us were starting to take the Pill, (Judith, ten years older, was ahead of us) reports of major side effects like blood clots began to emerge. In 1969, journalist Barbara Seaman wrote a book called *The Doctor's Case Against the Pill* that focused on women who had suffered strokes or died because of the Pill. Partly because of the media furor provoked by Seaman's book, Congress held hearings about the safety of the birth control pill the following year. After the hearings, the FDA ordered pill manufacturers to print patient package inserts detailing possible side effects of the medication.

In 1972, a woman in my college dormitory died of a Pill-related blood clot shortly after she graduated. The risk of dying from the Pill was less than the risk of carrying a pregnancy to term, but death seemed a high price to pay for contraception, particularly when there were old-fashioned barrier methods like the diaphragm and condom to fall back on. After 1970, there was a national decrease in the number of women taking the Pill, and we girls followed the trend. None of us took the Pill in medical school. We did not discuss our decisions with each other, so it is interesting that we all made the same choice. My 1972 edition of *Our Bodies, Ourselves* by the Boston Women's Health Collective doesn't advocate for or against the Pill, but details the controversy and suggests every woman weigh her options for herself. Many doctors advised women who did not have a regular partner to use other methods until they needed steady protection.

In addition to fear of blood clots, there were concerns about the Pill causing cancer or infertility. Women who go to medical school look ahead, and we were worried about possible unknown effects of the medication. Early on, it was evident that it took several months for women to start ovulating after they stopped the Pill. Women like Judith, who had taken the pill for a while, were advised to stop every few years to re-establish normal menstrual cycles. Eventually, studies showed that the women who did not resume regular periods after stopping the Pill were the ones who had irregular periods before they started taking it, but that was not clear in the early 1970s.

At about the same time, doctors started to notice an increased incidence of a rare type of vaginal carcinoma in young women. In 1971, an article in the *New England Journal of Medicine* established that the mothers of the women with the rare cancer had taken diethylstilbestrol or DES while they were pregnant. In the 1950s and 1960s the drug was widely prescribed to pregnant women to prevent miscarriages, although subsequent studies showed that it did not work for this purpose. DES was the first synthetic estrogen. If it caused cancer, why wouldn't the Pill?

The DES story made headlines all over the country. Since many mothers didn't remember whether they had taken DES or not, and many daughters, like Lorraine, had lost their mothers, women our age lined up to be checked at gynecology offices. It turned out that although my mother had not taken DES, I was born at a hospital where many women did take the drug. Since medical school I have been enrolled as a control in one of the largest studies of DES. Initially, I had to have a microscopic examination of my vagina to make sure I had no problems myself and fill out an extensive questionnaire. Every few years, they send me another questionnaire. These days there are questions about my daughter, too.

It is no wonder that the number of women in the country taking the birth control pill declined in the early seventies. When the Dalkon Shield IUD was introduced in 1971, one of the first IUDs marketed for women who had not had children, it seemed the answer to many women's prayers. It was a barrier method of birth control almost as effective as the Pill. By June 1974, when the manufacturer stopped distribution of the device, 2.8 million women had received one, Judith among them. It turned out that women with a Dalkon Shield were five times more likely than women with other IUDs to develop pelvic infections. All IUDs have a string hanging down through the cervix in order to pull out the device. Instead of one string, the designers of the Dalkon Shield used multiple filaments encased in a plastic sheath. This sheath served as a wick to allow bacteria from the vagina into the uterus, promoting infection. Many of the women who developed pelvic infections later found they had fertility problems related to scarring in the Fallopian tubes. Judith was among them. The rest of us relied on the diaphragm, which we knew had a higher failure rate than the Pill or the IUD, even when it was used properly. Implicit in this choice was the knowledge that we could easily obtain a safe, early abortion because of our privileged status as medical students. Karen, our psychiatrist, notes, "We felt comfortable with our bodies and empowered to negotiate with our partners about birth control methods which protected our health." Few women in the world, even today, can say the same.

Since we women spent ten to fifteen years of our reproductive lives sexually active and not on the Pill, it was no surprise to us to discover through my interviews that we all had abortions somewhere along the line. Two of us had them before medical school, at a time when women had to see a psychiatrist to certify that the pregnancy would be dangerous for the mother's mental health. "That was an unpleasant charade," Lorraine noted. *Roe v. Wade* was decided in 1973, the year we entered medical school. The other three of us who had abortions in training didn't receive any counseling, probably because our doctors assumed that we knew it all.

Not that anything would have changed our course. I knew I was pregnant right away. I could almost pinpoint the night. The diaphragm felt more there, as though it had lodged in the wrong place. And I was immediately sick. I told my husband my suspicion as soon as my period was late. There were no home pregnancy testing kits in those days, so I took a test at student health. Miles and I didn't discuss it much. We both felt it was my call. There was no way we could support a child with both of us in school. One of us would have had to drop out to work until the other one finished, years in the future. When I entered medical school, I had already decided that I would finish training, no matter what it required.

Many years later I asked a patient how he felt about learning he was HIV positive. He shrugged and said, "I was a player, and it caught up with me." It was the same for those of us who became pregnant using the diaphragm. The odds caught up with us. None of us belonged to a religious tradition in which abortion was considered a sin. If we had, we might have had more qualms about using the procedure as a backup for birth control methods we knew were all too fallible. Ruth remembers her mother helping arrange abortions for women "in trouble" in the old days. My mother knew two women in college who died after illegal abortions. We believed absolutely that we had the right to plan our pregnancies. It was not our fault that there was no perfect birth control method.

The day of the abortion, I was anxious and scared, but no more so than other days. I was used to doing things that other people don't do, like cutting up dead bodies and watching operations and examining naked people. The gynecologist who performed the abortion said, "We've all done it." I've always wondered whether she meant we women, or we women doctors.

At least two women in our class dropped out to have babies. They finished with later classes. Both of them had the advantage of an earning spouse. When I mention these women to my friends and ask why we didn't feel free to do this, they stare at me blankly. Don't I remember how every day was like treading water? Trying to hold a baby would have drowned us for sure. Even if the medical school accepted us back (which was by no means certain—as late as 1984, the chief of ob-gyn at Stanford tried to fire a resident who became pregnant, but had to yield to adverse public opinion) we did not feel we were strong enough to come back carrying a baby. The fact that a few women managed to have children in school then and more do it now does not change our personal assessment of our capabilities. We were at our limit.

The five of us also felt we would have been letting down other women if we dropped out to have children. Our women's history taught us that there had been another period when women were allowed into medical schools, a hundred years before. Women constituted 15–20 percent of medical school graduates in the 1890s, but only 2.6 percent in 1915. Male doctors, worried that there was an oversupply of physicians, influenced medical schools to stop the coeducation experiment. Men all around us, professors, relatives and even some classmates, predicted that we would drop out and have babies. We had no intention of proving them right. We did not want to see the door slam shut behind us because we did not honor our commitment. The personal was political.

Ten years earlier we would have worn skirts, ten years later we would have worn pants. Ten years earlier we would not have known about the Pill's side effects, ten years later most of our concerns had been answered by more research. Either way we would have avoided the Dalkon Shield. In our transitional time, we couldn't take anything for granted; we had to make it all up as we went along. Young women today see a range of comfortable shoes and pantsuits in the stores and visit Planned Parenthood clinics (which proliferated in the early seventies in response to federal funding) to obtain a prescription for a low-dose Pill. They can hardly imagine the effort we expended worrying about what to wear and how to safely avoid pregnancy.

Our experiences in the reproductive arena formed us as clinicians. We are skeptical of new miracle drugs and devices. We encourage our patients to make their own decisions about the risks and benefits of post-menopausal hormone therapy, the estrogen controversy of this generation. Studies show that female physicians are more likely to involve patients in medical decision making than male physicians are. We know firsthand what it is like to be a patient making decisions with limited information. Another reason we are "women doctors."

5. First Practices

"Woman must learn to contrive plots in which she is the actor, in which she struggles for control of her own destiny, slays her own dragons." (Carolyn Heilbrun, *Reinventing Womanhood,* 1979)

Ruth and David married in December of 1976, the middle of fourth year. By that time her parents were divorced. Her mother chose the Renaissance country club in Roslyn, New York, which Ruth describes as a Mafia hangout with red velvet on the walls: "think the Sopranos." It wouldn't have been Ruth's first choice, but she didn't feel very involved with the plans. It was all done long distance, over the phone. Her mother had scheduled a mother-daughter shopping trip to Bergdorfs for a wedding dress, but the salespeople were so arrogant, they left without buying anything. Ruth bought a Mexican wedding dress off the rack (the same solution I had reached a few years earlier). She didn't have an engagement ring because they were "out of fashion," but she says, laughing, that she's made up for that choice with jewelry purchases since.

A few days before the ceremony, she and David met with the rabbi his mother had recommended. "He was so paternalistic and old school. He was not going to marry me." So she found another one in the phone book. "Probably the first couple he had married in a long time who were both Jewish." They honeymooned in Hawaii, before the marriage.

Ruth and I were both a little surprised to marry young. We hadn't followed any of the rules in *Cosmopolitan* or *Glamour*, yet guys out there wanted us. Today the stars of Grey's Anatomy, surgical interns, are portrayed as sexy young women. In our day, the single women doctors debated when to tell a man about their professional commitment, because it was considered an obstacle to a relationship, like having herpes. Girls like us were "ball-busters." We watched, with amusement and pain, as women who were not in medical school threw themselves at our male classmates. We understood that to be a doctor's wife was a more suitable ambition than to be a doctor. When she was a medical student, Ruth had to tell her mother, "I'm going to BE a doctor" to stop her mother from urging her to marry a doctor. In the end, though, she was able to fulfill both her mother's ambition for her and her own.

During residency, we all reconstructed ourselves, professionally and personally. I remember planting a garden when I was a third-year resident. A friend came by and exclaimed, "I didn't know you were a gardener." I hadn't known either. I had never had time as an adult to find out. Anticipating a life with more sleep, I bought soft contact lenses my last year of training. Soft lenses had taken over the market since the last time I wore contacts, sophomore year of college. Motherhood put an end to illusions of rest, but that was still a year away.

At one point during my residency, I led an all-women's team. I was the resident, supervising two interns, a fourth-year student and two third-year students. One of my male colleagues, working in the ER, called us down to admit yet another scuzzy alcoholic. As we approached, he sang out to the patient, "Here come the girls!" The students looked to me to see how we should react. I burst out laughing and answered, "Yep, the girls will take care of you." My fellow resident may have been trying to disrespect us, but I felt so powerful without a man on the team, I didn't care. I only wish that someone had made the same announcement to the larger medical community before we entered practice.

One night toward the end of our residencies, we girls took ourselves out to dinner to celebrate. It was a fancier place than our usual choices, and we all made an effort. Dresses, makeup, jewelry, perfume. At the restaurant, we had to wait a few minutes to be seated. A lone man at the bar who had a few drinks under his belt looked over at us chattering in a mixture of medical jargon and English and asked, "Are you girls astronauts?"

We felt like it. Confident, attractive, and ready to take on the world.

No ceremony like a graduation marked the end of training. On my last day at the end of June, I signed out my patients to the resident picking up the service and walked out the door. Of our group, Judith and I finished first, because we left training right after residency. Judith felt she was too old for further training and I had not found a specialty that interested me above all others.

Ruth, Lorraine, and Karen all accepted the honor of a year of chief residency, in internal medicine, pediatrics, and psychiatry, respectively. The psychiatry residency was a year longer than internal medicine, so Karen emerged from training in 1982, two years after Judith and me. In the last year of her pediatric residency, Lorraine decided that she wanted to be a specialist. She says now, "I couldn't see myself, a single woman, childless, spending all day giving advice to parents on child-rearing." She considered pediatric specialties, but she chose a second residency in a separate field, dermatology. As a dermatology resident, Lorraine primarily saw adult patients: it appeared then that she was leaving pediatrics behind. Ruth stayed in internal medicine, but she sub-specialized in gastroenterology, which then required a two-year fellowship (It's longer now.) She also took a year off before her fellowship. They finished in 1983 and 1984, respectively.

When Judith finished residency, she was thirty-nine years old. I was twenty-eight. We had both been married six years. Compared to Judith, it might appear that I had plenty of time to have children, but I didn't feel that way. In fact, looking at the five of us, those with partners became mothers in our first year after training, while the two who married later became mothers as soon as they found partners. None of us sought to establish our careers first, although Lorraine had the opportunity to do so before she met her husband. We were ambitious women, and our ambition extended to our personal lives as well.

We wanted to prove that women could have a career and a family, just like the guys. We had kept up with the men in the medical training, but we had fallen behind in the family arena: their wives started to produce children during our residency. We understood that we would have to work twice as hard as the guys to be doctors and mothers, but we were not afraid of hard work. Judith had already started trying for a baby during residency. I waited until I was out of training six months.

The next step for Judith and me was to find a job. In my program, no one had spoken to me about life in practice, maybe because most people stayed on to do fellowships, maybe because I was a woman. I'll never know. Judith, at a private hospital in San Francisco, at least had an idea of the practice opportunities there. Some of our colleagues searched nationwide for the perfect position, but Judith and I limited ourselves to the Bay Area. Her husband had made partner in his law firm, and Miles was planning a gastroenterology fellowship at UCSF.

In 1980, the three choices for non-academic physicians in the Bay Area were public clinics, private practice, or Kaiser. Kaiser, a staff-model health maintenance organization, was and is the largest employer of physicians in Northern California. The jobs at the public clinics paid about half of a Kaiser salary, so the public clinic option only appealed to the most dedicated political types, or those with enough family money to ease worry about real estate prices.

Whatever we chose, in 1980, we still believed the decision was permanent. If we chose private practice, we did not expect to have our hospitals merge out from under us or to have to bargain with health maintenance organizations or preferred provider organizations for the privilege of treating their patients. If we chose Kaiser, we expected to be shielded from the economics of private practice, not to be forced to comply with the whims of MBA managers who had decided to "re-engineer healthcare." Our expectations were wrong. Already tired from negotiating a path through medical school and residency, we faced decades of change that would challenge our stamina and our values.

In retrospect, 1980 offered a hint of the impact the economics of health care would have on our lives. When the American Board of Internal Medicine sent us the scores for the exam Judith, Ruth, Miles, and I took in September, they included, as an experiment, a tally of how much we had spent to diagnose the hypothetical cases, and how much the average candidate who passed the exam had spent. I found the calculations vaguely interesting. I had been taught to avoid unnecessary tests for the patient's sake, but in our academic program no one had ever suggested limiting tests because they cost too much.

As it happens, the three of us who finished first all chose private practice.

Judith established a practice with Robert, a Chinese classmate of ours, in San Francisco. It was a verbal agreement, sealed with a handshake. They had trained in the same private hospital residency, where they were already members of the hospital staff. More important, the other physicians at the hospital knew them and their work. In those days before managed care dictated referral pathways, new doctors had to prove their competence and collegiality when they hung out their shingle. Needless to say, the medical community was overwhelming male.

Judith and Robert took advantage of the merger of St. Joseph's and Children's Hospitals to pick up used medical equipment. They sublet back office space from an orthopedic surgeon, who loomed as a sexist presence in front. Judith remembers him barking at his receptionist, Marjorie, when he wanted coffee, "Mar, cup!" To keep overhead down, Judith and Robert shared one employee.

Unfortunately, the list of equipment they needed in a primary care office was long. It started with the regular office stuff: stationary, a copy machine, electric typewriters, ledgers, telephones. For after-hours coverage, they needed beepers and an answering service. Then came furniture—chairs, desks, lamps, sofas, coffee tables, pictures, and carpeting for the waiting room. Then the medical supplies. Exam tables with stirrups for pelvic exams. Gowns, and paper for the table. Blood pressure cuffs large, medium, and small, a scale, an EKG machine, reflex hammers, otoscopes for the ears, ophthalmoscopes for the eyes, anoscope for the rectum, speculums for the vagina. A system to sterilize everything. Slides and spray fixative for the Pap smears. An emergency kit with syringes and drugs. Suture material, bandages, splints. They already owned stethoscopes.

Despite their cost-cutting efforts, the first year was difficult. Robert had counted on pulling in Chinese patients, but he spoke Mandarin and the Chinese community in San Francisco was largely Cantonese speaking. After six months, he decided to leave private practice for a corporate job. Judith could understand why, since she cleared only $13,000 that first year. Without her husband's financial support, she might have left as well.

Meanwhile, Judith was waiting for answers to the 700 letters she and Bob sent out across the country proposing themselves as parents for a private adoption. I posted one in the doctor's lounge at my hospital, for the obstetricians. Judith and Bob had been trying to conceive for years, while she was a resident, but her tubal problems from the Dalkon Shield IUD defeated them. In February of 1980, at the end of her residency, she traveled to New Jersey for a special tuboplasty operation. This was a last ditch effort to have a biological child. It didn't work. In the spring of 1981, they consulted a lawyer specializing in private adoptions and wrote the letter.

"I was afraid the pregnant teenagers would think I was too old to be a mother," Judith remembers. "Or would hold the fact that I was a doctor, not at home, against me." Practicing medicine was easy compared to waiting and hoping for a baby. Any phone call might be the lawyer with an interested birth mother. Then, once a birth mother chose them, any phone call might mean the deal was off. Judith was careful to ask about the mother's prenatal care before she accepted a baby. She turned down a baby from Maine when it turned out the mother was an alcoholic. Then they were in contact with a local mother, and had their hopes up until the baby was born without arms or legs. Although they decided not to adopt the child, Judith was able to tell us, some twenty years later, that the child had done well. She has kept in touch. She keeps in touch with the nurse who cared for her dying sister thirty years ago, too.

Unlike Judith, I had no desire to run a business. Kaiser would have been a logical choice, if I were planning to stay in the Bay Area, but my husband had signed up for specialty training, and the market for specialists was already tight around San Francisco. We expected to move after he finished his fellowship. Kaiser required three years of full-time work before partnership, and I wanted a baby before then. So when a black internist in Oakland offered me a salaried job in his practice, I figured it would tide me over until my husband's plans gelled.

Although many of the doctors in Oakland had trained at UCSF, the medical community was new to me. I was told that there were more black doctors in Oakland than anywhere except Atlanta, and I learned that referrals were made mostly along racial lines. At the time, three hospitals were located on "Pill Hill" in Oakland—Peralta, Merritt, and Providence. Maurice, the doctor I had joined, told me not to bother getting privileges at Peralta. They had only allowed black doctors on staff in the last few years.

Our primary hospital was Providence, which had a history of welcoming doctors and patients of all colors and income levels. Merritt, which was connected with a college of nursing, was considered more upscale. Although they were located across the street from each other, I could feel the difference between the two. The nurses at Providence were tickled to see a woman doctor and helped me from the beginning. The legions of white-capped nursing students at Merritt would jump up to offer their seat to male doctors who walked on the ward.

I was busy from the beginning, seeing Maurice's overflow patients and accepting patients from the emergency room. I quickly found that I knew my medicine. It was the politics that I found difficult. When a patient admitted so that I could rule out a myocardial infarction turned out to have life-threatening pancreatitis, I called in a surgeon to help. The patient was white, the surgeon was black. Without speaking to me, a white surgeon arrived, announcing that he was taking over the case because the family didn't trust the black surgeon (or me, was the implication). I signed off the case. I was not stupid enough to stay where I wasn't wanted with a desperately ill patient. That would be inviting a lawsuit.

By the end of a year, I was pregnant. My "morning sickness" lasted six months. Usually I vomited once after hospital rounds (the smells of blood, urine, and feces) and once before lunch. I lost ten pounds my first trimester. At twenty-nine, I was young to be having a first child, compared to other women doctors, but old compared to the national average. My biological clock was not ticking as loudly as Judith's, but medical school had taught me to go for what I cared about, that there are no guarantees in life. Lorraine says, "We put our emotional lives on hold during training. We had to focus on the things we had missed before we could get on with our careers."

We had missed a lot. The seventies were a glorious time to be young and free. If the sixties were about confrontation, the seventies were about lifestyle. Friends who were not in medical school lived abroad, partied, spent time on communes, dropped out of graduate school, hitchhiked across the country. We medical students worked sixty hours a week 1973–1980. We had the summer off after freshman year and that was it. Most of us had to work, then, too, to pay for our studies. As interns, my husband and I couldn't even schedule our two weeks of vacation at the same time. We had one week together, one week apart.

When we finished, we were in debt, unless like Judith and Ruth we were married to partners earning more than a resident's salary. UCSF was a tremendous bargain; tuition was only $325 a quarter for state residents. As adults, Miles,

Ruth, and I could establish state residency after a year, but four years of living expenses in San Francisco had mounted up. My husband also had loans from college, which he could defer only until he finished training. It is much worse now, when students can rack up $100,000 in loans over four years. Still, nearing age thirty, already in debt, and looking forward to a mortgage, there was no way we could recreate the carefree attitude of a recent college graduate.

Finally, unlike a soldier or a monk, who is at least isolated from the day-to-day world while he devotes his life to the fatherland or faith, we were right in the thick of regular life, delivering babies, caring for the sick and dying. In the clinic, we had to treat people our age with tan lines. In the hospital, where we spent most of our time, even the pediatric ward was home to the dying and chronically ill.

Here is an example of me talking to myself from a journal I kept as an intern. "Diana, coffee-colored, with blond streaks in her hair, eyes large with pain and helplessness. Her limbs are too weak to move her body, so she lies like a jellyfish in whatever odd position the last nurse or doctor left her. 'It hurted me real bad,' she whimpers. Which, Diana? The tumor growing in your belly or the part that has spread to your lungs? The three intravenous lines, the burning medicine in your vein, the vomiting, the hard x-ray table? Which, my little one? You are one year younger than I but you have your own baby. Your last, you tell me, because the drugs and the radiation have burned out your ovaries. Your husband has left you: what good are you to him? He is young, who can blame him? Only you, Diana, if you have the energy to spare." When Diana died, I remember thinking, at least she lived some of life outside a hospital.

While I was pregnant, I cared for a black woman in her early sixties who was dying of ovarian cancer. Her belly was swollen with cancer cells and fluid. In fact, the first doctor she consulted told her she was constipated. Although she had little education, on her first visit she looked me in the eye and said, "Dr. Martin, I am not constipated." She knew before I made the diagnosis. I admitted her to the hospital several times for chemotherapy, but the oncologist and the gynecologist saw little hope. As my pregnancy started to show, she joked that I would soon be as big as she was. I was embarrassed to have a belly full of life, when she had a belly full of death. She wasn't. She urged me to stay off my feet and took pleasure in my progress. When I left on maternity leave, we said good-bye: it was not likely she would last two months. She didn't.

My other twinge of sadness when my big boy was born, all ten pounds of him, was that there had been no news yet from Judith on the baby front. Then almost exactly a month later, she flew to North Dakota to pick up her first son. I remember us standing together, babes in arms, in her living room later that month, December 1981. It was raining, but inside the house her father had built, overlooking the bay, we were snug with our babies. How lucky and relieved we felt, that we had been allowed entrance into this female world of motherhood. In my worst moments of nausea, and the dark days of Judith's infertility, I had secretly wondered if we had asked for too much by becoming doctors. Whether our outsized ambition would keep us from fitting through the little gate at the playground.

Judith returned to work after a month; I returned after two months. There's no such thing as maternity leave in a small private practice. We had to get back to relieve the guys seeing our patients for us. I also had to worry about money. Miles had taken a year off to make money by working in emergency rooms, so that we could buy a small house. He was a gastroenterology fellow when our son was born, making less than I was. Judith and I returned to work full time, although I had more flexibility in my schedule than she did. I continued to nurse, pumping milk for the babysitter, until my son was about nine months old. Judith adopted her second son after six months. It had been so difficult to get her first child, she was afraid to turn down another offer.

We were always exhausted. Judith says, "I never sat down in those days, because I would fall asleep." She averaged four hours of sleep a night when the boys were little. Between night call and nursing, I probably averaged six. I had to excuse myself in the emergency room one night because my breasts were so engorged that I was afraid I would leak through my pads. I shut myself in the bathroom and squirted breast milk into the sink. It seemed pointless, to drag myself out in the middle of the night to admit a patient who chose to smoke cigarettes and drink alcohol, and would do so again, once his bleeding stopped. Meanwhile, my breast milk, my son's lifeline, was going down the drain.

Later, when Ruth went into private practice, we talked about how awkward it felt to hang out in the doctors' lounge, listening to conversations about golf and real estate and divorce settlements. When I was pregnant, well-meaning male doctors would talk to me about the joys of their young children, but typically these were their second families. They regretted how little time they had spent with the children from their first marriages, which often broke up after training. I remember thinking that a woman doctor doesn't have the luxury of a practice family. I had to get it right the first time, because there was no way I would have the energy to do it again.

Although Judith and I think of 1981 as the year our oldest children were born, it also turned out to be a momentous year in the history of medicine. A report of a few gay patients with an unusual skin cancer, Kaposi's sarcoma, heralded the AIDS epidemic. At first, as women, seeing mostly women patients in private practice, we had little direct experience with AIDS patients, although San Francisco was ground zero for the "gay plague."

When I came back from maternity leave in early 1982, I had a conversation with a pulmonary specialist who practiced at the same hospitals in Oakland. He had just spent a month as a visiting attending physician across the bay in San Francisco. He told me about the young men with pneumocystis carinii pneumonia who filled the ICU at the county hospital there. It was just a little over a year since I had passed my internal medicine boards, but I had never heard of that kind of pneumonia.

"And how did they do?" I asked.

"They all died." His expression was both sad and fearful. He was not afraid for himself—worries about contagion would come later—but for what lay ahead. The fact that this more experienced specialist felt impotent was the first time that AIDS scared me. It wouldn't be the last.

Soon, we started seeing, or recognizing, cases in the East Bay as well. It was years before we had a test to diagnose HIV, more than ten years before we had any drug besides AZT to treat the virus. We worked to prevent the complications, which prolonged life significantly, but each new diagnosis was a nightmare. The medical establishment initially insisted that these patients did not require specialist care, that every general doctor should be able to treat them. I believe this was an effort to decrease the stigma associated with the disease and to help those patients without access to specialists. But for those of us struggling to keep up with the new developments, as well as to cope psychologically with the deaths of so many young men, the pronouncements from the university medical centers seemed crazy. The treatment issues with these patients were just as complex as with cancer patients, who were treated by specialists. Finally, as new drugs came on the market for treatment in the 1990s, everyone agreed that it was unrealistic to expect most general doctors to manage what amounts to years of chemotherapy.

During the early 1980s, I wrote *How to Survive Medical School,* which was published in 1983. I used to get up in the middle of the night to nurse, and dash off a few pages. To finish it I spent a week's vacation at Lorraine's house chained to the typewriter while she was at work. The writing process allowed me to exorcise the ghosts of medical school, and the book became a "cult classic," if not a financial success. In a picture of our group taken in 1983, I hold a copy of the book in front of our smiles.

Judith's practice was financially successful after the first year. Another woman joined her, then a man, who self-destructed. He was an addict, who shot Demerol and played computer games in the office. After coping with this impaired partner, Judith was fed up, ready to consider something else. In 1984, she interviewed for a salaried job at the Kaiser facility in Richmond. The chief described the twenty-one-person practice (nineteen men and two women) as a "twenty-one-man" practice, which Judith did not find endearing. She also didn't realize that Kaiser wouldn't pay her salary for the afternoon a week she spent teaching at UCSF. Worst of all, on two mornings a week the doctors were required to see patients every five to ten minutes in urgent care. She decided to stick it out in private practice. By 1987, the practice had grown to five physicians, the income was more predictable, the night call was less frequent. And the boys were starting school.

I interviewed at Kaiser Hayward in 1982. Maurice had decided that he didn't want to pay me (and the other doctors he had hired) a salary anymore. We earned what we brought in, minus rent and overhead we paid to him. We were earning our salaries, but barely. I decided that if had to be in private practice, I would rather join someone else. Our practice styles were diametrically opposite. Maurice was only a few years older than I was, but he was from the paternalistic school, particularly with women. He told me not to bother counseling women about fitness because once they had children, women naturally slowed down and gained weight. When I explained to him that I was planning to nurse my baby, and turned down the formula the drug company had offered me, he asked me if that was quite safe. More important, as the big man in the practice, his billing always came first, with irregularities that worried me. I learned the hard way to check that the patients I had seen were billed under my name, not his.

My husband had received an offer to go into practice in Oakland when he finished, so I knew we would be in the area for a while. My preference, again, was a salaried position, and Kaiser seemed to fit the bill. I spent all day at Kaiser Hayward, touring and interviewing, on November 4. I remember the date because it was my son's first birthday, and I had hoped to get home early. My arrangement with Maurice was ending with the calendar year, I was still the primary breadwinner for a few more months, and I needed a job.

I didn't hear from Kaiser, so I called in early December. No one knew anything. Despairing, I agreed to join a classmate in private practice as of January 1. We had been making backup plans in case I didn't get the Kaiser job. Just before Christmas, Kaiser called and asked me to come for another interview. By that time it was too late. I had committed to staying in private practice.

My new partner, a man, was another refugee from Maurice's practice. He and I shared the same practice style and the same poor business sense. We knew our limitations, so we hired a consultant, who soaked us. We found out accidentally that we needed a business license from the city of Oakland. She hadn't bothered to mention it. Like Judith and Robert, we bought secondhand equipment and depended on one employee, but keeping the overhead down was a constant struggle. We accepted Medicaid patients and spent too much time with them. We learned why doctors ran Medicaid mills: you have to see a lot of patients at $16 a visit to clear the overhead. Astonished that most of the medical offices around us had no wheelchair access, we built a wheelchair ramp for ours. Later we figured out that doctors chose not to provide access to avoid the complexities of disabled patients. We didn't think that way.

The space we rented and later bought remains in my mind my one true office. We each had a consulting office in addition to the exam rooms. Mine was large enough for an old oak desk and two chairs for patients. Next to the diplomas on the wall, an abstract floral print with pink overtones declared my gardening passion. Years later, at Kaiser, I would have a consulting office again, a six-by-ten space I shared with another physician. There was no room for patients.

I had problems at home as well as at work. I was determined to make time for my son, especially since my husband, finishing his fellowship and starting in practice, was working long hours. I was always the one to get home to the babysitter and get dinner on the table. We lived in a two-bedroom house with no space for a nanny, even if we could have afforded one. I could not work the sixty hours a week my partner put in to reach close to the average internist's salary. Judith depended on live-in help, and worked much longer days, partly because her commute at rush hour was close to an hour, while my office was ten minutes from home.

As a specialist, Miles quickly started making more money than I did. His thirty-minute procedure was worth an afternoon of my time with patients. After my second son was born in 1984, I felt overwhelmed. Miles was cooperative, but equally tired. I thought that maybe he was depressed, because he seemed to be drinking more. It took a friend of his to point out that he drank too much, period. We had some major arguments before he admitted he had a problem and worked on it. Launching two practices and a family at the same time had taken its toll. In desperation, I sought a therapist again. This therapist didn't turn me away, but diagnosed major depression. She told me that I needed analysis, and I told her that I could only afford to come once a week. I begrudged the money, even for that hour, but I didn't want my children to grow up with a mother who was depressed.

I hung on in private practice, but I felt distant from most of the medical community. One of the necessities of medical practice is maintaining privileges at a hospital. At first, the hospital gives a new doctor provisional privileges, for a year. If the doctor is judged competent, the staff votes to change his or her status to active. A year after we started (my third year in practice) my partner and I received an invitation to the active staff dinner at Providence Hospital. The following year, only he received an invitation. When I called to ask why, a secretary told me that I was not on the active staff yet. I had been invited the previous year only because we shared a practice.

How could I not be on the active staff? I confronted the Chief of Medicine the first time I ran into him, on the stairs down to the same-day surgery suite. "It was an oversight. I promise, I'll bring it up the next time the executive committee meets." Perhaps. I felt like I had run a marathon and someone had "forgotten" to record me crossing the finish line.

This was an important moment for me, because I decided that I was never going to get credit for the work I did in medicine. In my mind, this "oversight" was the latest in the series of indignities I had suffered since I'd started medical school. Today I know that this kind of thinking is typical of depression. At the time, I vowed never to work so hard again.

Karen finished her chief residency in 1982. She decided to open a private practice and worked at the psychiatric emergency ward at San Francisco General Hospital to pay the bills while the practice grew. Kaiser was not a serious consideration for her because her training had emphasized talk therapy, not drugs. Kaiser benefits only pay for short-term, crisis-oriented therapy, which was not how she envisioned her practice. The influence of psychoanalysis was waning enough that Karen did not chose analytic training herself, but there was still a good market for private long-term therapy.

She hired a decorator for her psychotherapy office, someone recommended by psychiatrist friends. She laughs at herself now for thinking she needed a decorator. "The business part seemed so foreign. My fantasy was that the guys knew more about it than I did." She continued to attend meetings of a women psychiatrists support group that had started in residency. It still felt hard making all the decisions on her own. Some people paid for continued supervision of therapy, but she was tired of being a student.

The job at the hospital was stressful. Most of the patients were psychotic and acting out, so she depended on the psychiatric technicians and the police to help her restrain the ones she couldn't handle with words. Her relationship with the other doctors was collegial. Meanwhile, her private practice grew quickly because "everyone wanted a woman" and she had a good referral network of colleagues. Even her supervisors from training sent patients to her. It was very satisfying to find herself well respected in a sophisticated psychiatric community.

One of Karen's therapy supervisors, who had become a friend, introduced her to her future husband the first year she was in practice. Frank was a dentist and entrepreneur who lived in Los Angeles, although much of his business was in the Bay Area. A string of dental clinics had made him a wealthy man. When he and Karen met, he was only working one day a week as a dentist. The rest of the time he managed the clinics.

In his youth, Frank's father and mother ran a bakery in Los Angeles. Since he was the oldest of three boys, in the Jewish tradition, Frank had considerable responsibility early on, caring for his younger brothers and helping with the bakery business. Karen says he was ready to succeed his father at the bakery, but his father didn't want him to have to work baker's hours, up at 3 a.m. to start baking, selling all day. He told him, "Go to dental school. If you still want to be a baker afterwards, we'll talk." Instead, Frank used his business skills in dentistry. He also put one of his brothers through dental school.

Karen knew she was in love with Frank, and she wanted to have a family. Her biological clock was ticking. She was also very happy with her practice in San Francisco, and she enjoyed city life. She gave up the county hospital job after a year, partly because her practice was busier, partly because she was commuting back and forth to Los Angeles. She looked forward to her weekends with Frank, but the idea of living in Southern California made her nervous, even though she had grown up there.

Karen felt that she was just coming into her own as a psychiatrist, after all the years of training. If she moved to Los Angeles, she would give up her patients, her referral network, her colleagues, her friends. Frank, who was divorced, lived in a suburb of Los Angeles, Palos Verdes, and saw his three children every other weekend. He felt that he could not abandon them to move north. Karen suggested that they fly them up on his weekends. He thought that would be too disruptive for them. At one point, Frank and Karen broke up for a few months, largely because they couldn't resolve the issue of where they would live.

None of the rest of us had faced this type of stark, all or nothing decision between our personal and professional lives at the beginning of a relationship. One of Karen's close friends in the psychiatry support group, a woman who married during training, actually divorced her husband over a similar relocation issue, and remarried him when he was able to return to the Bay Area. She did not want to sacrifice her career to his. Eventually, Karen agreed to move to Palos Verdes, with the proviso that if she still felt marooned in the suburbs after a few years, they would move to Westwood or Beverly Hills, areas that felt more urban and sophisticated, more like San Francisco. Karen says now, "We were told that we could have it all, but someone has to compromise when there are two careers. I felt that I couldn't give up this chance for a husband and family."

Karen speaks wistfully of the evening she and Frank attended the Black and White Ball in San Francisco. The ball is a special summer occasion, when party-goers eat drink and dance their way through downtown venues like the Opera House, City Hall. The festivities last well into the night, with people literally dancing in the street. Everyone dresses in black and white: "I wore a black dress with big white polka dots." (It makes me smile to imagine petite Karen in big white polka dots.) The ball symbolizes the life Karen left behind when she moved to Los Angeles.

Karen and Frank married in June of 1985. Lorraine and Judith attended the event. The service was in a synagogue, the party was at the house. They'd built a platform over the pool and invited 130 people. Frank's corporate plane flew some guests down from the Bay Area. To the rest of us, Karen's new life had a fairytale quality. She'd found a rich man who whisked her off to an elegant suburb of Los Angeles. We didn't think about what a difficult transition she faced.

Frank offered to move to a new house, but after looking around, they settled in the same house that he had shared with his ex-wife. He was only four and a half years older than Karen, but most of his friends had school-age children like his (thirteen, eleven, and eight when they married) or older. In their suburb, there was no population of young single women seeking therapy that Karen could draw on for patients. In order to develop a practice, she had to take call in the hospital again.

The whole culture of psychiatry was different in Los Angeles. In the Bay Area, psychiatrists still practiced therapy. In LA, even in private practice, they already focused on prescribing medication, while psychologists and social workers provided therapy. In San Francisco, Karen had worked with women who had eating disorders, but in Los Angeles the treatment of anorexia nervosa was "franchised." The Rader Institute dominated the market. Karen worked enough with them to figure out that she wasn't comfortable with their model of treatment. Above all, she felt that she was a "career woman" in a neighborhood of housewives. She said that even Frank's mother was afraid that she wouldn't take care of him properly, that a woman doctor wouldn't be nurturing enough.

It upset Karen that she was the one who had to give up her life, that she was the one to do all the accommodating. Frank introduced her to people he knew in the medical community and helped her establish her practice, but she missed the prestige she had left behind. "I knew he was doing all he could, but I was still angry." I can hear the frustration in her voice over the phone two decades later. Karen may be soft-spoken, but she was ambitious, too.

The situation didn't improve until her first daughter was born. Through her, Karen started to make her own friendships, with other mothers. It wasn't the same as the professional success she had enjoyed in San Francisco, but she felt she had her own identity again. Palos Verdes became her home, as well as Frank's.

Two months after her daughter's birth in 1986, Karen went back to work three days a week. Her life looked balanced, although she, like all of us, felt the strain of multiple roles. Her work schedule was predictable, her husband was available, and she was happy to be a mom. It was still stressful to be on call, even from home, so when an opportunity came up for a job without after-hours responsibility, she took it.

Judith remembers 1987 as the year a woman called her up and introduced herself as the case manager for one of Judith's cancer patients. "I'm here to make sure that you don't over refer." On our side of the bay, my partner and I were facing the same kind of intrusive management from HMOs. We had been forced to hire another staff member to sit on the telephone to obtain authorizations for specialist treatment. It seemed like every week another health plan thrust a contract under our nose to sign. Each plan claimed that our patients would leave if we didn't join that panel of doctors. We did not have the knowledge to evaluate the contracts, and we couldn't afford to hire a lawyer to evaluate them one after another. We balked at signing the "capitated" contracts, through which we received $10 a month per patient no matter what the patient needed. At $30 an office visit, what were the odds a patient would require more than four visits a year? How many patients from that group would we have to see to break even? We didn't know.

As the business of medicine became more difficult, I found myself wanting to spend more time with my children, which made me less productive, a vicious cycle. When I should have been at business meetings learning how to read the contracts, I was at home reading bedtime stories. In 1980, colleagues had assured me that medicine was going through "a bad patch" which would soon be over. By 1988, when I left, Mom and Pop practices like ours were an endangered species. Lines from my journal in 1986 speak to my state of mind at age thirty-five:

Grey and bald we falter
The horizons inch closer
More twilight, less sun.
Consequences mount
As youth recedes.
The children tame us.
The patients die.
We grow slow.

I made the decision to have a third child and to close my practice at the same time. When I floated the idea in conversations, before I decided, people said I was committing professional suicide. They said I just wanted a girl, and I would be disappointed when I had another boy. They said we would regret the decision because of the financial strain. Everyone was so negative, I returned to therapy for a few months. My therapist pointed out that on a strictly financial basis, it wouldn't make sense to have children at all.

My younger sister and I were pregnant at the same time. Her son, born four months before I delivered, had a heart murmur that seemed more ominous at birth than it has proven to be. Lorraine was in the midst of her infertility crisis. My journal from that time is full of apprehension and concern for "my third son." What hubris to have another child when I already had two boys. When the baby was born, the pediatrician said, "Congratulations. Another healthy baby. And a bonus—a girl."

I never worked full time as a doctor again. Karen, already committed to a part-time practice, opted for a third child also. Though our children seduced us, the roots of our ambivalence about medicine can be traced back to third year.

When I complained to another doctor mother, a plastic surgeon, about how hard I found the transition from the pace of the doctor (fast, goal-oriented) to the pace of small children (slow, meandering), she replied, "You spend too much time with them." Yes, that was the problem. A few years later she gave up practicing medicine entirely, though, overwhelmed by the balancing act. I was amazed that she could walk away from all that training. In fact, after fifteen years raising her children and earning an MBA, she retooled and returned to practice.

My partner joined another group on Pill Hill for a year, then followed his heart to a small town in the mountains, where he didn't have to cope with HMOs.

By 1988, Judith was the only one of the three of us who had started in private practice still in the same place, doing the same thing. When Ruth and Lorraine opted for Kaiser in 1983, the grass looked greener on that side of the fence. Yet they didn't live happily ever after either.

6. The Kaiser Alternative

"Work smarter, not faster."
(Kaiser slogan in the eighties)

When Ruth started at Kaiser San Rafael, she almost enjoyed the forty-five minute commute north of the city. All the traffic was headed to San Francisco, while she drove out into the country. Into suburbia, really, but the one-story businesses splayed along Highway 101 were car dealerships and furniture stores that didn't fit in the city. It felt open to a city girl. The medical center was a low-slung building set behind a curved driveway flanked by trees. It was the kind of California she recognized from TV, more relaxed than San Francisco.

Inside the facility, there was more space and light than in the city hospitals. A small group of young doctors worked well together. The senior gastroenterologist was a man she knew and respected from training. He served on the clinical faculty at UCSF and set an academic tone in the department at Kaiser. She would sit with him and go over cases at the end of the day. One of the great pleasures of a Kaiser practice is the variety of patients in the system. Since there were only two gastroenterologists at San Rafael, and patients could only see Kaiser doctors, Ruth had a large referral practice right away.

We had been surprised that Ruth did not pursue a career in academic medicine after her chief residency. She had the political connections within the institution as well as the smarts to stay on. When she quoted from the medical journals on rounds, everyone else fell silent, because she always knew more. As a GI fellow, she felt she owned the role of woman star. In fact, when another woman joined the program a year behind her and promptly got pregnant, Ruth resented her. The woman miscarried at five months and Ruth says that she "felt responsible" for the loss of the baby

Recently, I asked Ruth why she left the university. "I wanted to have children." Even with her energy, she did not see how she could combine an academic career with children. She was always anxious and fiercely competitive, as a resident and a fellow. She has an easy laugh, especially if the joke's on her, but when

78

she talks medicine, she slips into another gear, her voice low, fast and earnest. When we were residents together, and she presented a case, I dared not let my attention wander, for fear of losing the thread of her argument. At night, her husband used to find her sleepwalking in the living room, sure she had been called for a patient. She knew herself well enough to recognize that if she stayed in the cutthroat atmosphere of academic medicine, she would drive herself crazy.

Perhaps Ruth learned this in the year she took off between her chief residency and her fellowship. She studied French that year. She spent two months traveling in Europe, then stayed home reading novels and going to movies. She talks about the delight of food shopping without time pressure, smelling the fruit, and picking out perfect vegetables. We all nod. When we left training, there were so many simple pleasures to rediscover. Taking a job at Kaiser was a step down in prestige, but she was thirty-four years old, looking at the big picture. Her husband had been at Kaiser Hayward for years, and he was satisfied. She was pregnant by her second month at San Rafael.

The Kaiser system is complex. The Permanente Medical Group employs the doctors, who care exclusively for patients with Kaiser insurance in Kaiser hospitals and clinics. The three branches of the organization, the Permanente Group, the insurance plan, and the hospitals, are separate corporate entities.

When Kaiser began as a pre-paid medical group in California in the 1940s, to provide care for the men who worked in the shipyards, it was completely out of step with the rest of the medical community. The local medical societies barred Kaiser doctors from membership because of their "socialist tendencies." Doctors who taught us at the university still looked down on Kaiser in the 1970s. Since an ambitious, hardworking physician could make more money in private practice, what kind of doctor would trade potentially higher earnings for regular hours and a salary? Someone who valued time off and group practice, like Ruth's husband, who had joined the Permanente Medical Group after residency. And women.

The Permanente Medical Group did not have separate "maternity leave." The thick Permanente Policy Manual in the brown loose-leaf binder said, "Women physicians may use accrued sick leave and leave of absence without pay for maternity purposes." As an internist and gastroenterologist, Ruth also accrued time off for working at night and on weekends. Nevertheless, she estimates that only one of the three months she took off was paid leave. "If I had been single, I would have had to return to work right away."

The problem with treating childbirth as an illness is that women doctors have children early in their career and most illness, in men and women, occurs as people age. The youngest women physicians finishing residency after going straight through the shortest training are turning thirty. With the chief residency, her fellowship, and the year off, Ruth was thirty-four. Women don't have the time to accrue the sick leave available to a man who has his first heart attack in his forties, or prostate cancer in his sixties.

Ruth found returning to work full time more difficult than she had expected. She would start crying when she left the house, cry over the Golden Gate Bridge and up Highway 101, and stop crying when she parked. (She told people that she had allergies, to explain her red, swollen eyes.) She didn't expect to feel such an intense pull to her son. At the same time, she didn't feel that it was okay to give less than "110 percent" at work. She wanted to be the best.

The word "intense" rings a bell for me. We are all intense, the five of us. To some extent, we have channeled our intensity in different ways, but we are intense mothers as well as intense doctors. The intensity was a well of energy we drew on to survive our medical training. Out in the world, it has been a mixed blessing.

In 1986, Ruth had an opportunity to transfer to Kaiser San Francisco. The change saved her the commute, and brought her to a hospital with interns and residents, closer to the academic model she cherished. Today she says she wishes she had stayed in the Kaiser system, that it would have been an easier lifestyle than the private practice she joined later. I prodded her about this, because I remembered hearing issues about night call that she doesn't mention at first. She thinks back, sifting through her memory. "Well, I guess things weren't perfect, because I remember looking around for another job ..." The story emerges.

When she was pregnant with her second son, the other two gastroenterologists at Kaiser San Francisco left. In those days, the subspecialists in medicine had to be on call for general internal medicine as well as their specialty. The chief of medicine recognized that Ruth could not be on call for GI every night, so he arranged for someone from another facility to alternate call with her. Pregnant, and facing every other night GI call, Ruth asked if she could be excused from the general internal medicine night-call rotation until she returned from maternity leave. The chief refused. Ruth laughs as she remembers patients she saw in the middle of the night urging her to get off her feet. But she's not laughing when she tells me her second son was two pounds smaller than her first son, which she ascribes to the stress of that pregnancy.

Ruth returned to Kaiser, but when she received an offer from a prestigious downtown private practice, she jumped ship. She tells me that if she had known how hard establishing her reputation again in private practice would be, she would have stayed at Kaiser. Perhaps. A friend who stayed at Kaiser once offered the opinion that it was a system which suited the type B personality, a more easy-going, competent, but not brilliant doctor. Ruth was always type A. That intensity again.

Lorraine accepted a job at Kaiser Oakland several months before she finished her dermatology residency. She spent the last few months of her training in Chicago, with a pediatric dermatologist who became her mentor. The field of pediatric dermatology was in its infancy in those days. Her mentor had started the first journal of pediatric dermatology a few years before Lorraine met her. Twenty-two years later, Lorraine became the co-editor of that journal. She also helped write the first board examination in the field.

Only Ruth and Lorraine report having had a mentor. Karen had a group mentoring experience, with women faculty members in the psychiatry department who met regularly with the women residents. Judith and I found that one of the disadvantages of a larger field like general internal medicine is that the training is more anonymous. And we were all wary of the older men. Many of them could not see our ambition and our intellect across the gender boundary. We recognize the character Jeremy Browning in Allison Pearsons' novel, *I Don't Know How She Does It*: "There are some men who will always prefer to deal with another man, any man, rather than a woman, and Jeremy Browning is one of them. I can see him struggling to place me: I'm not married to him, clearly I'm not his mother, I didn't go to school with his sister and I'm sure as hell not going to bed with him." Ruth's mentor was only a few years ahead of her in training. Lorraine's was a woman.

Prior to her experience at Children's Hospital in Chicago, Lorraine had seen at least as many adult patients as children in her dermatology residency. In her job at Kaiser, she would be treating mostly adults. Ironically, she now feels the seeds of her discontent at Kaiser were sown before she even started, during those happy months seeing exclusively children in Chicago. Adults often see dermatologists for trivial complaints. Children almost always see their pediatrician first. If they are referred on to a pediatric dermatologist, it's for more than a pimple.

Some of us were tethered to the Bay Area by our spouses, but Lorraine felt as a single woman, an orphan in the world, that she could not uproot and establish herself on the "open market," a phrase that terrified her. She had been born at the Kaiser Oakland facility, and it felt like home to her. She didn't look at any other job and didn't negotiate. "I didn't feel I was anything special." None of us did. Ruth and Karen, who had served as chief residents in addition to their outstanding performances in residency, could have used those honors as negotiating points. Lorraine was double-boarded, in pediatrics and dermatology, which reflected two more years of training than other dermatologists. Later, when I joined Kaiser, I didn't bring up my experience as a justification for higher wages. Judith admits that she was so grateful to be accepted in medical school at her advanced age, she had mentally pledged to do substantial charity work. None of us recognized what we were worth.

Lorraine traveled to Europe for the first time at the end of her residency. She felt that she was finally fulfilling her mother's dream for her, to get out and see the world. When she moved to Oakland, she and I took a Thai cooking class together. With two little boys at home, I already knew the course had limited utility for me, but as a single woman, Lorraine looked forward to experimenting more in the kitchen. We all had hopes for a broader "real life" after training.

At Kaiser Oakland, Lorraine joined a group of five dermatologists who all sat in the "bull pen," a large common room. There were no separate offices. Since she was used to the conditions of residency, this physical arrangement didn't initially strike her as strange, but she soon tired of hearing a couple of her colleagues on the phone with their brokers. She liked the chief, an older Chinese doctor with a thick accent, because he was academically oriented and a good clinician. He had a soft spot for her also, because she reminded him of his cherished daughter, a physician who had trained at Harvard Medical School. After a year, Lorraine was able to arrange one half day of pediatric work, but the majority of her patients were adults. Still, she enjoyed getting to know the pediatricians and the geneticist at the facility. They, in turn, appreciated that she was willing to come to the hospital to help with puzzling pediatric patients.

In 1985, Lorraine bought her first house. She borrowed the down payment from her uncle and paid him back with interest at market rate. Although she was a proud home owner, buying a house by herself was a bittersweet accomplishment. Lorraine says today that she had always felt that if the right man came along, she would give up medicine if necessary to be with him. "You all looked shocked when I said that," she says to us later. Well, I was surprised to hear her say it so nakedly, but I knew she had longed for a man to share that house in Oakland.

She was the only woman in the dermatology department at Kaiser Oakland. Her colleagues were cordial. As her reputation increased, however, she started to suffer from "adverse selection." Other doctors would refer difficult patients to her, patients who had significant dermatological problems and needed time. She began to be aware how unevenly the work was distributed. Two of her colleagues were very cynical, brusque with the nurses and the patients. They tended to drop the ball when serious problems came up. The chief's style was not to counsel them (maybe he had given up), but to take care of any issues which arose himself. It annoyed Lorraine to watch these male colleagues getting paid, getting bonuses, but not pulling their weight.

When another woman from UCSF joined the department, life improved for a while. Then the chief was forced to retire because of his age (she thinks he was 70), and Lorraine was appointed chief, with his blessing. Although she was a logical choice, as a rising star, some of the guys who had been in the department much longer than her four years were annoyed. A few of them transferred to other facilities. In the Kaiser system, administrative work has special appeal, because it is one of the few ways to get a break from the assembly line of patients, every ten minutes in dermatology. "Aerobic medicine," Lorraine calls it.

It was difficult to hire replacements for the doctors who had left. At one point fifteen dermatology positions were open in Northern California, largely because the Permanente Group was not offering enough money compared to private practice. (Eventually, they raised the starting salary and the positions filled.) The long waits to be seen led to unhappy interactions with patients and with doctors in other specialties. As chief, Lorraine fielded the phone calls. While she enjoyed meeting other department chiefs and talking about substantive issues at administrative meetings, the additional workload made for longer and longer days.

On the personal front, there was good news. She started dating a man she had first met when he was a resident in the internal medicine program at Kaiser Oakland. Sam had been a resident when Lorraine was an attending because he had detoured through the counterculture before entering medical school. He lived on a commune in Northern California. They were the same age. Unfortunately, when he had been at Kaiser, he was married. Lorraine had noticed him, but she wasn't willing to have a relationship with a married man. It was a matter of self-respect. Sam had also noticed Lorraine. He was impressed with her poise and competence when she gave medical grand rounds. "At the time, I was married to an entirely different kind of woman, and Lorraine's professional stance was very attractive."

After his residency, Sam did an infectious disease fellowship in Los Angeles. Lorraine had heard that he and his wife had separated, so when she was in Los Angeles visiting family she called him up. On their first "date" he came over to her grandmother's house for a family dinner, with Lorraine's sister and cousins. In the course of the conversation, Lorraine mentioned that she had heard that the house that her family once owned in Oakland, the house she had grown up in until seventh grade, had sold for several hundred thousand dollars. Another example of the inflationary California real estate market. Sam didn't say anything at the time, but when they went out for coffee later, he revealed that it was he and his wife who had lived in Lorraine's childhood home and sold it when they divorced.

The coincidence of the house kick-started their relationship. Both of them wanted children, and Lorraine's biological clock was ticking. At this point, we girls had known each other for a dozen years. Lorraine had been dating all that time, guys we liked, guys we didn't like. This one understood how special she was. Sam took a job at UCSF when he finished his fellowship. They were married in 1987. Lorraine couldn't face a big ceremony without her parents, so they were married by a rabbi in their house, with only Sam's parents, her siblings, and a couple she had known from childhood as witnesses. She was disappointed that her uncle and aunt, who she had hoped would serve as surrogate parents, attended an event for a friend instead of her wedding.

Lorraine and Sam hosted a reception afterwards at the U.C. Berkeley Faculty Club. The redwood building, designed by Bernard Maybeck in 1902, is nestled into a grove of trees on the campus and recalls the gracious ease of a barely modern world. It was a clear, sunny day, and guests wandered from the great hall to the courtyard, from a klezmer band in one space to a quieter scene around a coffee bar in another room. Lorraine's younger sister's boyfriend sat down at the piano and offered a few tunes. It was not a giddy, twenty-something affair, but a moment of deep happiness.

A few months after the wedding, they tried to start a family, only to find out that Lorraine had entered menopause prematurely at age thirty-seven. It seemed hardly credible, that her reproductive system would conk out within months of their marriage. Yet Lorraine's experience, like Judith's, is common to many women of our generation. They did not meet partners with whom they wanted to have children until late in their reproductive lives. I once asked Lorraine if she regretted her abortion in light of her later infertility. She was surprised at the question. She never wanted to have a baby for the experience of childbearing, as some women do. She wanted a family. Other women of our generation, who had partners and delayed childbearing by choice, believing their options unlimited, felt betrayed by the rhetoric of the women's movement.

Those were grim days for Lorraine, at work and at home. She hired a new woman dermatologist, who immediately became pregnant. It was a struggle to take her Clomid, give herself Pergonal injections, and face this perky colleague all day. I, too, was pregnant with my third child, who was born in April 1988. Lorraine told me she didn't resent me as much, because she knew my life wasn't perfect, which I took as a compliment. Yet many of our conversations ended with her in tears.

The practice situation at Kaiser was worse and worse. Lorraine bitterly quotes the slogan of the day, "Practice smarter, not faster." She wanted to scream, "I'm not practicing this way because I'm stupid." She enjoyed the more complex patients who represented an intellectual challenge, but those patients take more time than people with acne. She didn't approve of how other doctors manipulated the system, booking non-existent patients, for instance (a well-known, strictly forbidden way to slow the assembly line.) As chief she wanted to set an example. Her hopes of having a referral practice with more pediatric dermatology had not materialized. As an administrator, she saw that there was no mechanism in place for other Kaiser facilities to pay her for seeing their pediatric patients. The budget for each facility was separate. Oakland paid her salary, so she had to see Oakland patients, mostly adults. (Kaiser has since figured out a way around this roadblock, and a pediatric dermatologist at Oakland currently sees regional referrals.)

Lorraine began to have physical symptoms of stress. She felt short of breath, as though she was drowning. She developed neck pain that required physical therapy. "Emotionally, I was a wreck."

The last insult was the nursing strike at the end of 1988. The doctors had to cross the picket lines and work as nurses for "over a month" as she remembers. Lorraine was assigned to the telemetry unit, monitoring cardiac rhythms of patients who had been hospitalized for heart problems. Her last experience with adult cardiology had been in 1977 as a fourth-year medical student. She was terrified that she wouldn't recognize a life-threatening arrhythmia. "It was all about money, with no regard for patient care." As the daughter of Communists, Lorraine considered herself a "union maid," so she was profoundly conflicted in her management role. Crossing the picket line each day took an act of will.

One of the aspects of practice at Kaiser that had attracted Lorraine in the first place was the collective spirit. She no longer felt a part of that. Her disillusionment with the system coincided with the failure of her fertility treatments. When she was offered a position in the dermatology department at UCSF, it didn't matter that the pay and benefit package was less than Kaiser's. She wanted out.

Ruth, Judith, and I, in fields that required significant weekend and night call, immediately had to face hard choices between family and career. Already, in these early years, I started slipping off the career track, working less as a doctor, and writing. Ruth and Judith chose the sixty-hour-a-week lifestyle. Karen was able to achieve a better balance, partly because of the nature of psychiatry, partly because her husband was past the career-building stage, and partly because her vision of a doctor was more flexible than ours. Lorraine, to her chagrin, had more childless years to devote to her career, years that would pay off later. She could not predict the comfort of that future success when she was trudging back and forth to the fertility clinic, though.

Those of us who were in the Bay Area would get together at least once or twice a year over dinner. Ruth and Judith met for lunch because they both practiced in the city. Judith and I took the boys to the park together. Lorraine and I jogged together once a week. Occasionally we had family potlucks, including husbands and children. It is hard for women to keep up with each other when their child-bearing is out of synch—we all felt that at times. My children used to resent Lorraine for taking me away from them, but I didn't let them complain in front of her. She figured it out, ten years later, when her children grumbled about my visits.

On the other hand, our meetings were a safe place to discuss our anxieties about the children and our lives. No one in our group would give us the lecture we feared hearing from other women, "Well, if you would just stay home." Or, "if you didn't work so much." When I mentioned the idea for this book to one doctor's wife, she snapped, "Who would want to read about a bunch of spoiled, rich women!" From our perspective, of course, it is the stay-at-home doctors' wives who look like spoiled rich women. I remember how amazed I was to find that women who didn't hold a job employed au pairs so that they could lunch and play tennis. A friend told me recently about a young woman pediatrician she met walking back from their lunch hour at Kaiser. She asked her if she walked for exercise at lunchtime. "Oh, no," the pediatrician replied. "I go home to do the laundry." Yes, that's what we did in our "time off."

As we inched our way over this new terrain of motherhood and practice, we were aware of the structural changes in the practice of medicine during the late eighties and early nineties. No medical system was immune to the speedup of patient care and the advances of technology. Men who had never learned to type had to learn to use computers. Surgeons had to learn to operate with laparoscopes through tiny incisions. Hospitals merged. Private practices combined in order to achieve greater bargaining power with insurance companies. At Kaiser, there were rumors that the Health and Hospitals branch wanted to dump the Permanente Medical Group and find doctors who would work for less. Men complained that it was like working two jobs, keeping abreast of the changes. For us, it was job number three.

7. Corporate Medicine and the Good Girl Double Bind

"A study by Wikler (1976) comparing male and female university professors found that students expected women professors to be warmer and more supportive than male professors; given these expectations, proportionally more women professors were perceived as cold." (Arlie Hochschild, *The Managed Heart*, 1983)

When I was new to Kaiser, I tried to attend most of the noon conferences in the Department of Medicine. In the nineties, Kaiser launched a technology initiative to put the medical records online. Each time the system was modified, there was a computer lecture. We doctors, eighty internists, sat in rows, in uniform, white coats with the Kaiser logo on the sleeve and our names embroidered on the breast pocket. We wolfed down the white bread sandwiches that came wrapped in a plastic package with a piece of fruit and wrote patient notes in the morning charts we'd brought from clinic while we listened. The speakers were eager techies, who'd grown up with computers. On one occasion, a young man urged us to "play around with the system in your free time." A male colleague seated next to me, an older man I hardly knew, turned to me and said quietly, "If I had that much free time, I would have sex."

I laughed so hard (but so silently) that I choked. He patted my back.

At another of those Kaiser lunches ("Indigestion City" because eating fast while receiving yet more bad news tied our stomachs in knots), our Physician-in-Chief reported to us the findings of a health care advisory organization Kaiser had hired to "seek a new patent." The idea was that we had saved all the money we could save by keeping people out of the hospital, and now we had to figure out other ways to cut costs. The consultants predicted (suggested?) that soon hospitals would (should?) only have intensive care units. Patients who did not need the one-on-one nursing and technology of the ICU would be sent directly to nursing homes. "This is the future," the boss told us. "We have to adjust to it."

We internists looked at each other, convinced that anyone who could make such a prediction had no experience with the level of care in actual nursing homes, or the unpredictable course of illness. What would happen to the patient unfortunate enough to come to the emergency room in the middle of the night with severe pneumonia? If he didn't need a breathing machine yet, he would be shipped to a nursing home? And if he deteriorated, he would be shipped back to the real hospital?

I was told that those consultants went bankrupt in the next few years. That particular threat did not come to pass. Yet sometimes it felt, both at Kaiser and in private practice, that we doctors had to keep one hand free to ward off the crazy ideas that the business people pitched day after day. They had time to dream this stuff up, because they didn't see patients. They made more money than we did without getting their hands dirty. It was particularly irritating, at a time when the organization was asking us to work an extra clinic per week for the same salary, the equivalent of a pay cut, to hear how much money they were shelling out for consultants.

Our medical careers have almost exactly coincided with the triumph of the corporate model in health care. The business model includes managed care, which came early to California, where we practiced. But it is more than managed care. It is the idea of looking at patients as "consumers" to be attracted in the marketplace, the struggle for the "efficient" delivery of care, the implementation of technology to manage health care systems, the creation of practice guidelines. The new business practices changed the Kaiser system, which had been "managed care" since the 1940s, as much as they changed private practice.

Today, when Kaiser has emerged as the most viable HMO in California, it is easy to forget how scared they were in the 1990s when they had lost money two years in a row. Anxious to retain the patients they had, struggling to improve their market share, the administrators at Kaiser felt forced to adopt the practices of other HMOs. The cost-cutting mania was "the race to the bottom." "Someday," we were told, "employers (who purchase health insurance) might care about quality. Today they only care about cost."

Male doctors sometimes blame "docile" women for the erosion of professional autonomy that accompanied many of these changes. This seems hardly fair, since the health care inflation of the nineteen seventies, when there were still very few women in practice, provoked the "economic reform" of the nineteen eighties. Even as greater numbers of women arrived on the scene, we were not in positions of power.

On the other hand, as feminists, we women were receptive to some reforms. We were sympathetic to the consumer movement that sought to even out the balance of power between doctors and patients We did not wax nostalgic about the "golden age of medicine" in the sixties when patients had no say in their care. Most of us had personally suffered under that system, because no sexually active woman can avoid seeing doctors, the way men can. There are the yeast infections, the urinary tract infections, the birth control questions. In the sixties, the system worked for the doctors but not for the patients. After almost thirty years of market-dictated reform, we have a system that doesn't work for anyone.

From the moment that we set foot in medical school, our generation of women explicitly acknowledged the emotional work of practicing medicine. We cared about how patients felt, what they understood. In training, this put us at odds with our instructors, who were scornful of the "touchy-feely" side of medical practice. Only Karen, as a psychiatrist, felt she had permission to speak about emotional concerns of patients without risking her professional stance. Once we started in practice, we found that there was a tremendous pent-up demand for doctors who practiced in a more egalitarian, less authoritarian style. The explosion of health care information, in the media and on the Internet, has only increased the number of "consumers" who want to negotiate their health care.

All this new information has transformed the practice of medicine, particularly the primary care specialties of pediatrics, family practice, and internal medicine, where women doctors are concentrated. As risk factors for chronic diseases like diabetes and coronary heart disease have been identified, medical organizations and the government have encouraged doctors to counsel their patients about preventive care. The recommendations that these groups make are published for laypeople, who come in asking about mammograms or cholesterol.

In the past, doctors could count on a group of well patients who visited for a yearly physical and were satisfied with "a clean bill of health." A quick and easy visit. Today, doctors must counsel patients about risk factors for disease, even if they are perfectly well. It takes as long to convince healthy people that they need a doctor to look into their rectum with a tube as it does to explain a pill that lowers blood sugar to new diabetics. A recent study in the *American Journal of Public Health* estimated that it would take up to seven hours a day for a family practitioner to provide all the preventive services recommended for the patients in their practice. There would be little time left over to treat illness.

By the 1990s, the politics of "patienthood" had changed so much that the demands of the women's health movement—respect for the patient and safety information about drugs—looked tame. AIDS activists showed no deference to physicians. Why should they, when we doctors were flailing in the dark? Gay men with AIDS set the agenda for their visits. Patients with other diseases and the legions of the worried well soon wanted to fashion doctors in their own image. Anatole Broyard, who suffered from prostate cancer, wrote in 1992, "My ideal doctor would be my Virgil, leading me through my purgatory or inferno, pointing out the sights as we go." I have read Dante's *Inferno*, and Virgil did not repeat his tour every fifteen minutes.

Compare Broyard's extravagant plea with the spare concern of William Carlos Williams, the doctor-poet of the turn of the century who inspired me in the 1970s. "I don't care a rap what people are or believe. They come to me. I care for them and either they become my friends or they don't. That is their business." Williams listened to his patients, but he was a no-nonsense guy. What would he have made of Kaiser's slogan, "Give the patient what they want when they want it"? Would he list his hobbies for the marketing folks so that patients could choose a doctor with similar interests?

All doctors cope with the new higher consumer expectations, but patients assume that women doctors will try harder. Studies of doctor-patient communication suggest that by and large they are right. Women doctors tend to spend more time with patients and engage them more in decisionmaking. Some evidence also suggests that the health outcomes of patients of women physicians may be better. Patients of women doctors receive more preventive care like mammograms and Pap smears. A recent study showed that the risk for poor blood pressure control was two times higher for diabetic patients treated by male physicians compared with those treated by female physicians.

At the same time that the information explosion and the emphasis on prevention fueled the demand for services, new business practices emerged that focused on "productivity," or seeing patients faster. A Kaiser internist ten years older than me told me that at first, he had seen only fourteen patients a day. We saw that many patients in a morning. In private practice, health plans speeded up doctors by decreasing the amount of money paid per visit. If a doctor wanted to keep earning the same amount, he had to schedule more patients. One of my neighbors, a "consumer" who left Kaiser, unhappy with what she felt was assembly line medicine, soon began to complain that doctors in private practice were running their offices more like Kaiser. She was right. Everyone was paying the same business consultants to tell them what to do.

Ironically, we women who represented the changing face of medicine found ourselves allied with the more conservative, older doctors, who also had philosophical (and sometimes physical) trouble with the universal speedup. These older male doctors could complain without being perceived as "soft." But when any physicians voiced opposition to the shenanigans of the business consultants, our ideas were dismissed. In private practice, business consultants told doctors that our opinions were not credible because we were blinded by greed. At Kaiser they told us that doctors just couldn't understand business, as though we were genetically handicapped.

In those days, the consultants used to brag about the fact that they had no health care background. According to them, my practice was like a car dealership: my skill set was a product line that consumers wanted. We doctors didn't know whether to laugh or cry at this analysis. Somehow in business school, they'd entirely missed the point that doctors like me spend a good proportion of our time coaxing people to do things they don't want to do, like exercise, take their medicine, cut down on sweets. We also try to discourage the irrational use of medication and technology. Antibiotics don't help a cold, and an occasional headache that goes away with aspirin is not an indication for a brain scan. Are there New Age car dealers who talk customers out of buying cars?

Once the pharmaceutical companies started direct-to-consumer advertising in the early nineties, the problems escalated. The relentless promotion of "lifestyle" drugs may produce a better-informed consumer, as the drug companies maintain, but it also fuels demand for medication. I remember the day that Renova was approved: I received phone calls from three patients requesting prescriptions. I had no idea what Renova was, so I called the pharmacy (this was before we had the Internet at work) and learned it was a face cream for wrinkles. Then, I had to call three patients back, explain that it wasn't on the formulary yet, and that I didn't know whether it would be. This was not how I had imagined spending my time when I was in medical school.

In addition to the normal emotional work of a practice, the changes in the delivery of health care brought new challenges in terms of anxious, upset patients. The gatekeeper role was particularly onerous. Judith and I, as primary care doctors, coped with the authorization and referral end of the new system. We had to add staff in private practice, significantly increasing our overhead. But the worst part was finding ourselves in an adversarial relationship with some of our patients. In medical school, we struggled to find our doctor identity; in practice we struggled to come to terms with it as it was redefined.

Ruth and Lorraine, the specialists, found themselves at the other end of the problem, trying to triage the many requests for appointments. Since the HMOs wanted the primary care doctors to handle as much as they could by themselves, they tried to keep only enough specialists on provider panels to handle problems that truly required a specialist. There were not enough to satisfy everyone who felt they were too important or their problems too unusual to be treated by a general doctor.

Patients who were used to the kind of insurance that paid for the doctor's visit, any visit, resented the restrictions of the new HMOs. Kaiser patients accused the primary care doctors of trying to save money if we were reluctant to refer to a specialist. Even if we provided the referral, the patients complained about waiting the several months it took to be seen in orthopedics or dermatology. Since the insurance executives were not on site, even at Kaiser, we doctors and our staffs bore the brunt of the complaints.

When patients did complain to insurance companies, they were told that if their doctor felt that it was an emergency, the doctor could call the consultant. This was a passive-aggressive way of dumping responsibility for the rules onto the physicians. As the insurance companies well knew, we primary care physicians couldn't possibly advocate for every patient who felt deserving of a sooner appointment, like the patient who told Lorraine that her plantar wart was an emergency.

All doctors have to cope with disgruntled patients, but patients feel freer to vent their feelings to a woman, and expect more in the way of service. A friend of mine at Kaiser in suburban Walnut Creek met a patient whose first words to her were, "I want to see my fucking chart." They didn't teach us how to come back from that opening gambit in medical school.

The sociologist Arlie Hochschild wrote a book called *The Managed Heart* about this kind of "emotional work." She studied male and female flight attendants to see how they handled the service aspect of their job. Among other things, she found that, "Third, and less noticed, the general subordination of women leaves every individual woman with a weaker 'status shield' against the displaced feelings of others. For example, female flight attendants found themselves easier targets for verbal abuse from passengers so that male attendants often found themselves called upon to handle unwarranted aggression against them."

Lorraine noticed that when she left Kaiser and moved to an academic position at UCSF, the level of complaining from patients decreased dramatically. At Kaiser, she was another dermatologist in a system patients suspected of achieving savings at their expense. A week later, at the university, practicing exactly the same way she had at Kaiser, with patients who had waited just as long as the Kaiser patients had to be seen, she was an "expert." Suddenly her "status shield" was a lot stronger.

We girls who chose medicine deliberately turned away from the "Coffee, tea, or milk" kind of work a flight attendant performs. We assumed that if we made it through the arduous, masculine training process, we would have the same "status shield" as a man with an MD. At the same time, our feminist background prevented us from dismissing demanding patients out of hand. This then, was the "good girl double bind": our willingness to listen combined with a weaker "status shield" left us vulnerable to frustrated patients as well as to colleagues eager to avoid emotional work. One woman doctor at Kaiser reported that a new patient told her that one of the male doctors had advised the patient to transfer her care to that particular woman doctor. "She likes to talk," he said. Even if that particular woman doctor did like to talk, she faced the same time constraints her male colleague did.

We also emerged from training just when "science" appeared to endorse the "natural differences" between men and women. In her 1982 book *In a Different Voice*, psychologist Carol Gilligan argues that women are by nature more caring than men are. Gilligan intended her work to be a feminist refutation of Freud's contention that women were "less mature" in their moral development. Unfortunately, as Barnett and Rivers argue in their book, *Same Difference* (2004), Gilligan's work has stereotyped women anew. Yes, women listen more and are better at reading emotions, because generally we have a lower status in society than men do. It is critical that a slave know what the master is thinking: his life depends on it. Studies don't show that women in positions of power retain these behaviors.

Yet many people are relieved to redraw boundaries between the sexes with a thick black line. Men and women are so different, they come from different planets, says John Gray, the author of *Men Are From Mars, Women Are From Venus*, first published in 1993. Although the bestseller gives relationship advice and has nothing to do with men and women doctors, by reinforcing stereotypes about the behavior of men and women it highlights the gender divide.

An article about women doctors in the magazine *Medical Economics* (Sept. 2005) starts out, "And if stereotypes are at least partially grounded in fact, women have long been seen, and see themselves, as nurturers." The article then quotes the author of a study of women physicians, Klea D. Bertrakis: "Female physicians have more female patients and female patients report themselves as being in poorer health than males and require more time." Yes, our experience exactly. Only the corporate model considers doctors interchangeable. It doesn't recognize that sicker patients triage themselves and are triaged to the "nurturers."

Judith told me that when she was new in practice, she used to get many referrals from one particular emergency room doctor. At first she welcomed these referrals, as a practice builder, until it dawned on her that he only sent her women patients with complicated medical and psychosocial problems that she had to unravel. When she confronted the physician about her suspicion, he told her, "I send them to you because you're so good with these people." Her answer was, "I may be good with them, but don't send me any more." She feels strongly that this version of what Lorraine called "adverse selection" helps account for the income differential between men and women doctors in primary care.

For a while at Kaiser Oakland, there were two rheumatologists, one a man, the other a woman. The woman was convinced that the advice nurses sent the more difficult patients to her. They and the administration stonewalled her. Our chief called her a "whiner." Yet when the unit manager left, he admitted to her that she was right. He probably felt safe to tell the truth at that point because he was moving to Ohio.

Occasionally, our male colleagues recognize our efforts. A male doctor once told Ruth that she was doing a service to the community by coping with a particularly neurotic group of patients, who are so fragile they can't cope with the preparation for the procedure. "The nurses know they are mine when they need a pillow between their legs to lie on their side and cry when the IV is started." The doctor told Ruth that she couldn't retire, because no one else would accommodate that group of patients.

I once accompanied an oncologist to a family meeting to explain a young man's terminal illness. After the oncologist rambled on in pure medical jargon for about ten minutes, he asked if the family had any questions. It was clear that they hadn't understood anything he said. So I repeated the message in plain English, checking for comprehension along the way. In the end, they understood, and thanked us both for our time. As we walked out, the oncologist turned to me and sneered, "That's why we have women in medicine."

Even without selective triaging of patients, there were structural reasons that women doctors of my generation faced a different job from men. Because women go to doctors more than men do, and want to see women doctors, our practices filled faster than the men's. A Group Health administrator estimated some years ago that the average woman starting in that HMO filled her practice within a year, as opposed to three years for a man. This problem should get better with more women in practice. But in our day, women worked harder, sooner.

Women are widely acknowledged to be savvier health care consumers than men. They also tend to function as health care managers for their families. If men have practices with 60 percent women, and women have practices with 75-80 percent women, the women doctors will be fielding more questions. A medical group recently ran an advertisement in the San Francisco Chronicle to attract Medicare patients to their HMO.

The picture in the ad shows an older couple, and the text reads, "Her job is to choose a Medicare health plan. His job is to say, 'Yes, dear.'"

A host of illnesses, many with a significant psychiatric component or that require ongoing education, are more common in women, so having a higher proportion of women patients changes the provider's job. Type II diabetes, for example, is more common in women. A family practitioner told me that when her health plan compared her practice to that of a man with a comparable number of patients, she found out she was seeing twice as many diabetics. Irritable bowel syndrome, the most common GI diagnosis, affects three times as many women as men. The rheumatic diseases are almost all more common in women, especially the controversial ones like chronic fatigue and fibromyalgia. And certain difficult psychiatric syndromes, such as somatization disorder, where mental distress is manifest through endless physical symptoms, occur almost exclusively in women. Depression is twice as common in women. Seventy-five percent of patients with borderline personality disorder are women. Men have more substance abuse, but the problem there is usually getting them to admit it, not frequent visits.

Women doctors don't want to ignore the emotional work of practice. It is part of the job. The problem is that we don't get credit for our extra work. In 2000, the *Journal of General Internal Medicine* published a study of patient satisfaction with their primary care providers in the Kaiser system. It found that female patients who chose a woman doctor placed a higher value on communications skills and were less satisfied with their medical care. They were less satisfied even though the female doctors used more communication strategies that the patients valued. An editorial accompanying the article suggested, "Nevertheless, even good performance may not be sufficient to meet the high expectations of female patients for their female doctor, particularly under tight scheduling constraints typical of managed care." The male patients of the same women doctors were very satisfied with their care. If insurance companies use patient satisfaction surveys to determine compensation, women may suffer in comparison to men, even though we are carrying more than our share of the emotional load.

The irony is that we women doctors sometimes have difficulty empathizing with our women patients. Our education, our relative financial independence, our success in a male profession, give us a different perspective. It amazes me that women with chronic fatigue syndrome, whose chief complaint is lassitude, would assume that they would have a special connection with women doctors, who live on adrenalin and caffeine.

A pediatrician turned psychiatrist told me the following anecdote to highlight the emotional distance she feels from other women. At her daughter's preschool, a child ran into the street and was almost hit by a car. But he wasn't. The other mothers told the story over and over, pulled their own children closer, kept comforting the child's mother who was having difficulty collecting herself to drive home. My friend, who had cared for critically-injured children who had actually been hit by cars, did not see a near miss as the same tragedy her friends did. She's a doctor, after all.

The idea of women as "natural nurturers" echoes the historical role of women doctors in maternal and child care in the early twentieth century. Ellen More, in her history of women doctors, calls this the era of "maternalist medicine," during which middle-class women doctors worked to improve conditions for working-class women and children. The question that was debated then, and remains alive today, is whether women have a separate role in medicine. Are we clustered in the specialties that deal with women and children because of external barriers or because we see this as our mission? Are we better at coping with psychosocial issues because of innate ability or because we face them more often?

This question is more urgent for some women doctors than for others. Ensconced in the pediatric world, which is now 50 percent women, Lorraine practices with men who are comfortable caring for women and children. For women obstetricians and gynecologists all the patients are women, and the busy private practitioner can benefit financially from a larger patient load. A childless gynecologist confided to me that she found pregnant women disgusting, because they were so "fat," but she had a huge private practice of women who assumed she was more empathetic than a man would be. The idea of women's medicine can appear to offer a "separate but equal" solution to making sure our biological differences are appreciated. In salaried corporate medicine, however, if the women gynecologists are double and triple booked while the men have empty slots, the women are working harder for the same pay.

One of the most successful family practitioners I know, someone who started when I did, but survived for twenty-five years in private practice, limited her office hours to three days a week from the beginning. She took on a partner who works Mondays with her and the two days she doesn't work, so one of the doctors is in the office at all times. Neither of these women have children. They just accepted from the beginning that they were "women doctors"—doctors who coped with more psychosocial problems and needed time to recharge. They are at the low end of the earning curve—a male colleague with children left their practice because he needed more income—but they earn enough for themselves.

Most of the women I know, like myself, kept trying to squeeze into the standard model, convinced that there was something wrong with us because it didn't fit. In corporate medicine, there is only one model.

The transition to corporate medicine has been stressful for everyone in our generation, men and women. But studies show that women doctors feel more pressure in managed care systems than men do. This is attributed to our practice style: we "like to talk" and are so empathic that we have difficulty setting limits. Health care analysts offer gender stereotypes to explain our stress, but do not consider whether the same gender stereotypes may influence the job we face. A telephone advice nurse at Kaiser told me that the nurses prefer to work with men doctors, because they receive fewer calls. As far as I know, this question hasn't been studied, but the observation lines up with the gender roles. A good Daddy is busy, better not to bother him. A good Mommy is endlessly available.

Some women try to fight the system by dropping skills that distinguish them. I don't know anyone who has changed gender to avoid the "nice" stereotype, but a Latina friend refused to see Spanish-speaking patients because English was her first language (although she spoke good Spanish), and translation took extra time. The woman who "liked to talk" planned to let her geriatrics credential expire, because old people slowed her down. In corporate medicine, any extra skill that attracts patients is a liability. As long as people assume that women doctors have a skill set that is different from that of men, we will face different expectations in the workplace.

I didn't consciously choose hospital or urgent care work to duck the expectations of patients attracted by the "nurturing" stereotype, but I like seeing a wider social cross-section of patients, including people, like most men, and working class people, who avoid the doctor until they fall ill. Men don't mind seeing a woman doctor if they have a problem, but they rarely choose one of us from a list for their regular doctor. My male patients typically bonded with me during an episode of acute illness and stayed on.

When they are sick, men and women are pleased to find an empathic doctor, rather than disappointed that the doctor doesn't want to be their therapist or their new best friend. Even Karen, in psychiatry, where the relationship is the sine qua non of the encounter, finds that she enjoys seeing patients who do not often seek therapy, Latinos and working class men and women, in her workers' compensation practice.

The medical profession shies away from studying and discussing the effect of gender stereotypes in the workplace. If we don't talk about it, maybe it doesn't exist. Partly this is because the culture of medicine discourages "whining." A flight attendant may not lose face asking a man for help, but a woman doctor does. How can we say that we are as tough as men if we complain? Our generation of women felt that we were on probation for years into our careers. We didn't go looking for trouble.

Other industries are far ahead of us in this discussion. In 2005, the Catalyst group, a research and advisory organization, issued a report sponsored by General Motors, called *Women "Take Care," Men "Take Charge" :Stereotyping of U.S. Business Leaders Exposed.* They summarize their findings succinctly: "Even though analyses of more than 40 studies of leadership, spanning more than 15 years, fail to support their perceptions, women leaders are still judged better at 'caretaking' leader behaviors and men better at 'take charge' behaviors." Women in business see demolishing stereotypes as a way to break through the glass ceiling. For most women doctors, once we are out in practice, away from academia, there is no career ladder to climb, but job satisfaction enters into our decisions about how much we want to invest in our careers.

Young women today view medicine as a "normal" career choice, instead of a challenge to gender roles, as it was in our day. That's a welcome change. But our colleagues and our patients still notice whether it's a man or a woman in the white coat, and the cultural norms for the behavior of men and women remain distinct, no matter what the setting. Our lived experience in medicine in a time of rapid change suggests that gender stereotypes are resilient and sneaky, like viruses that mutate too fast to allow the development of a vaccine. Molly Carnes MD, co-director of the Women in Science and Engineering and Leadership Institute at the University of Wisconsin, describes "a mountain of research in the social sciences that fairly consistently shows that due to unconscious assumptions that we all have, women and the work performed by women consistently received lower evaluation than men and the work performed by men. And this is true no matter whether the evaluators are men or women." A mountain changes the weather on the ground, even when people don't see it.

8. Doctor Mothers

"These ask not, 'Is she capable?' but, 'Is this fearfully capable person nice? Will she upset our ideal of womanhood, and maidenhood, and the social relations of the sexes? Can a woman physician be lovable; can she marry; can she have children; will she take care of them? If she cannot, what is she?'" (Mary Putnam Jacobi, MD "Shall Women Practice Medicine?" *North American Review*, 1882)

When I worked in the Kaiser system, I attended a workshop for women doctors about finding a balance between motherhood and doctoring. The woman who facilitated the workshop asked us to stand up. "Raise one hand if you're a doctor. Raise a foot if your husband works outside the home. Raise the other hand if you have children. Raise the other foot if you help care for elderly parents, or commute more than a half hour a day, or care for someone with a chronic illness." Soon all of us had to sit down because we had no limb left to support us. Our leader continued, "This exercise demonstrates that your life is impossible. Don't let people tell you that you need to be more organized. Women doctors are the most organized people on earth. You are stuck in the middle of a stalled social revolution, where the women have gone to work, but the men have not stepped forward to share the caretaking at home."

I started crying, silently, behind my glasses. It was the first time I had heard someone admit that working harder, working smarter, wasn't going to help. What I had long understood, however, was that once my husband and I had children, they were my responsibility. If we were introduced as two doctors at a cocktail party, he was asked what his specialty was, and I was asked what I did for childcare. I am not going to discuss why this is so, or whether it is fair. Nor am I going to rant about why our country refuses to fund high-quality, affordable daycare for all working women. I will point out, however, that we are among the most affluent mothers in the country, and simply finding reliable care, of reasonable quality, was not easy.

Why did all the women in our group decide to have children, knowing full well how they would complicate our lives? Ruth says that most of the impetus toward becoming parents initially came from her husband. The rest of us felt more internally driven. In Karen's case, her husband already had children and didn't feel a compelling need for more. She wanted them: stepchildren weren't enough. Lorraine says that at times she wishes that she could have been the kind of woman who didn't need to prove herself by having children. She bitterly contrasts the adulation that she receives at work as a dermatologist and mentor with the sarcasm and lack of respect she often faces at home from her teenaged twins. Judith and I, as general doctors, had a different problem. For years we felt that we faced the same challenges at home and at work: demanding individuals with unrealistic expectations who couldn't or wouldn't take responsibility for their own lives.

Ironically, I suspect that we all became mothers for the same reason that we ended up in medical school. Like the Marines, we wanted to be all that we could be. It would have been impossible for me, after spending all those years learning about the miraculous process of procreation—the DNA that codes our sex; the hormones that create a boy or girl in utero from a unisex model; more hormones that kick in at puberty to start sperm production and egg release and kick off that drive (oh, that drive!) to couple; the transformation of a muscle the size of a fist to a womb with a placenta to nourish the baby ; the exhilaration of the moment of birth, which we had experienced as medical students; the profound relationship of the nursing mother and infant; and the complexities of child development—it would have been impossible for me to say, "Oh, no, thanks, it sounds too hard."

Here was a chance to participate in the fundamental biological destiny of the species, to create and rear the next generation. When Judith and Lorraine found that the creation part didn't work for them, they still approached the experience of becoming parents and raising children with energy and enthusiasm. Even when we felt lost in a dark cave, during our children's developmental trials and adolescence, the scientists in us found enough light to marvel at the process.

We embraced motherhood, even though our own mothers had not necessarily valued the role. Once when my mother was bemoaning her lack of opportunity as a black woman, one of my sisters pointed out that she had raised five daughters with very little help from my father. "That's not worth anything!" my mother snapped. Her tide of bitterness has ebbed with age, but she still believes that circumstance robbed her of a chance to make her mark on the world.

Ruth's mother, trapped in an unhappy marriage, also did not find fulfillment in raising children. (Ruth's parents divorced when she was in medical school.)

Her mother went back to teaching when Ruth was in second grade, which improved their family life because she had been so frustrated at home. Although Ruth, the oldest, has two younger brothers, she feels that her mother's focus shifted elsewhere once she was working again.

Lorraine, who lost her mother in college, can only speculate about what their relationship might have been as two adults. As a teenager, she felt that her mother didn't understand her. People outside the family loved her mother's energy and told Lorraine how lucky she was to have such a dynamic role model. But Lorraine felt that her mother saw her as not quite as pretty, not quite as accomplished, as her older sister. In the fifties, parents didn't put as much effort into trying to see each child as an individual, particularly in larger families. Lorraine was the second of four, and I was the middle of five. We remember moving en bloc, as "the kids."

Karen, too, feels that her mother didn't "get" her when she was growing up. She says that her mother was too strict when Karen was a teenager. "She didn't trust me, despite my good grades. She thought I would go bad somehow." Karen's mother was in her early twenties when Karen was born, and Karen attributes her mother's anxiety to a lack of confidence.

All of us, except Judith, experienced tense mothering from strong women. In some ways, I think our uneasy relationships with our own mothers guided us to demanding careers. There wasn't an obvious fallback position for us, as there might have been for women who felt more confident in their innate mothering skills. Although Judith's mother taught her daughter to trust her instincts, in a way the rest of us never could, Judith's parents also divorced, and Judith herself had a marriage behind her by the time she enrolled in medical school. None of us believed that domestic contentment just happened. We expected to have to work to be good mothers, especially with our other obligations.

As doctors, we also could not wrap ourselves in the kind of optimistic maternal fantasies that many women embrace, the same way they dream about their weddings. Our time on labor and delivery disabused us of the rosy picture of "natural" childbirth. We saw Cesarean sections and babies with congenital defects and birth trauma. We saw women who had trouble nursing, developmental delay, child abuse, childhood leukemia. We cared for girls of thirteen who were pregnant and others who had anorexia. Aside from nurses, most other women don't have the kind of in-your-face experience with what can go wrong with children that doctors have.

When we girls gathered in my living room to discuss the parenting chapter of our lives, everyone expressed trepidation. We wanted to describe the strains of the mother-doctor role as truthfully as possible, for younger women and for our children. Yet we knew this chapter would be painful. We quickly agreed that the mother role was more of a challenge than the doctor role. Karen pointed out that her work was predictable in a way her children never were. Ruth says she doubted herself more as a mother, worrying and second-guessing her decisions. Lorraine felt more vulnerable, that her kids routinely upset her equilibrium in a way that patients, even difficult patients, couldn't.

The only one of us who now says that she felt equally confident as a doctor and a mother is Judith, who faced some of the toughest parenting issues with her boys. She attributes her faith that everything would work out to her mother, "who was the best possible mother for me." The rest of us suspect that Judith is speaking at least somewhat with the benefit of hindsight when she talks about her boys, but then we can't imagine what it would have been like to grow up with "the best possible mother for me."

Judith and I started our families within a month of each other, she by adoption, me by giving birth, but Judith completed hers six months later by adopting a second son. Her husband tried to talk her out of taking another child so soon, but she wanted two children and she had learned how difficult the adoption process was. This time, she met the birth parents and loved their sense of humor. She told her husband, "I've got to have this kid."

When I heard the news, I couldn't believe it. Six months after my son's birth, I was barely able to keep up, exhausted from nursing and working. Judith didn't have the physical strain of pregnancy and nursing to cope with, but two babies at different developmental levels may be even more work than twins. I wonder now if she was intoxicated by the surge of self-confidence that marks the end of medical training—if I made it through that, I can make it through anything. In those days, many people would have said what Judith had already accomplished was impossible: who had ever heard of a woman starting medical school at age thirty? She wasn't going to be deterred by anyone telling her that another child after six months was too much. She promised her husband that she would stay home two days a week. She hired live-in help. She had a plan.

Unfortunately, the plan foundered because her babysitters were not up to the task. Initially, she hired au pairs, German and Dutch girls who wanted to be in the United States, but couldn't cope with the children. One of them didn't like to change diapers. She left dirty diapers and wipes on the floor. Another would fall asleep, blaming her drowsiness on the antihistamines she took for allergies. One day when Judith came home early, she found that the sitter had wedged a pacifier in the four-month-old baby's mouth by tying a diaper around his head.

Judith was untying the diaper when the sitter walked over and picked up the older boy by his arm. Judith fired her on the spot, canceled her patients for the next day, and worked frantically to find a new sitter. Another time, she found the younger boy with a black eye, allegedly from falling down the stairs. "It was lucky no one was killed," she says now.

The kinds of near misses with the children's safety that Judith describes are every working mother's nightmare. She spoke matter of factly, but a chill came over the rest of us as we listened. Intellectually, we know that a moment's inattention with a toddler can result in tragedy, no matter who is there, but when it happens on the babysitter's watch, it feels like it's Mom's fault, not Dad's or the parents'. I heard of a woman doctor whose baby fell off the changing table while he was under the sitter's care and hit his head. He developed a seizure disorder, and the doctor never returned to work. Certainly in Judith's house, she was the one who was supposed to accommodate her job to the children. In part, this was a financial decision. A general internist starting out does not make as much money as a partner in a corporate law firm. It doesn't make sense for the high earner to cut back. Unfortunately, the more the low earner circumscribes her career to be available for the children, the less likely it is that she will ever reach her earning potential. Judith and I both struggled with this financial Catch-22.

The older boy was a poor sleeper, up two and three times a night. Judith's husband was helpful when he was there, but he worked long hours and traveled frequently. She found it difficult to manage her practice from home on the days she tried not to go in. She was on call for the office via beeper, and emergencies happen. She remembers a particularly difficult day when the boys were eighteen and twenty-four months, and an elderly patient had fallen at home. She was trying to assess the patient over the phone with the boys screaming in the background. After that, she started going in half days on her days "off," so she was effectively working full time, counting night and weekend call.

After two and a half years of struggling with the au pairs, Judith found an older Vietnamese woman who had raised twins and knew which end was up. She stayed with the boys for ten years.

Judith, Ruth, and I always had to cope with night and weekend call. While Lorraine carries a beeper regularly, true emergencies are rare in dermatology. Some psychiatrists have to take call, but Karen is one of the many who don't. Today people take cell phones for granted. They like staying in touch. Living tethered to a beeper for medical emergencies is not the same. Judith, Ruth, and I could never ignore the page—it might be a nurse from the ICU where the patient just had a cardiac arrest, or the emergency room doctor announcing a patient vomiting blood. We dared not finish reading the story or making love or eating lunch before answering. Of course most of the time, the problem turned out to be much less dramatic. A nurse calling to ask if the patient could be changed from a clear liquid to a solid diet. A patient calling from home because of leg cramps. But the effect of interruption after interruption is relentlessly destructive to personal life. In the days before cell phones, we had to stay close to a phone or stop the car to find a pay phone. More than once I have pulled off the freeway into an unknown neighborhood and called from a telephone booth outside a liquor store. If we didn't answer the page, the hospital could call the police to roust us out. (It happened to my partner once when he fell asleep with his beeper downstairs, and his cat knocked the phone off the hook.)

The man I joined initially in private practice told me once that he didn't mind being on call. "There's nothing I do that I wouldn't be near a phone anyway." He didn't hike or swim, as I did. He didn't go to concerts or the theatre. I thought of the doctor I knew who put his beeper in a plastic bag and strapped it to his chest when he went windsurfing. It was difficult to be on call as a parent, but some of us had personalities that strained against the duty well before we had children.

We were all in call groups, so we didn't have the beeper every night. One weekend a month was about average. Miles was also on call about one weekend a month, different weekends from mine so that we could cover the children. Judith's husband had long hours as a lawyer, but he didn't take call. Ruth's husband had to spend about a night a month at the hospital, but when he was home, he was not attached to a beeper. The nights and weekends add up. It was my toddler son who pointed out to Miles and me that "Some parents don't work on weekends." He said it so hopefully, I felt sure he thought he was bringing us new information that we could act on immediately. Why couldn't we stay home, if other parents did?

It was clear from an early age that Judith's older son Dan "had issues," as Lorraine likes to say. At first, it was hard for us girls to tell whether it was a question of a temperamental mismatch, a more physical boy in a bookish household, or deeper behavioral issues. He had difficulty in school, and by fourth grade his parents wanted him to see a therapist for behavior problems, but he refused to go. They found an art therapist who came to the house, but that didn't help much.

Meanwhile, Judith's husband Bob was assigned to a long-running court case in Southern California. For six years, from the time their sons were eight to when they were fourteen, he commuted to Los Angeles during the week. He left on Sundays and returned on Fridays. Judith says that she felt pressure again to curtail her practice, but that she didn't think that staying home more would help, because it was his Dad that Dan missed. Dan had always been closer to his father than to his mother. The younger boy was thriving in school, and the contrast between the two was painful.

In sixth grade, Dan crumpled up a test in a teacher's face. Judith and her husband agreed to withdraw him from the private school. He insisted they call him by another name. He started painting swastikas on the wall at home, took all the knives in the house into his room, and changed the lock on his bedroom, so no one else could enter. At this point, his parents did not feel safe with him in the house. They decided to enroll him in a therapeutic community boarding school in Colorado that cost $70, 000 a year. He stayed there for two years, ages twelve to fourteen.

I remember Judith telling us about Dan's expensive school at a brunch at Ruth's house. In those days we girls saw each other as a group only a couple of times a year, so we always had a lot of catching up to do. The rest of us were shocked to hear how difficult the situation had become. We all had boys except Karen, and we wondered if our boys could turn on us like this. We wondered if any school could rescue such a troubled child, even a school that expensive. Judith spoke quietly, without tears.

Only recently did I ask Judith the obvious question, "Did you consider quitting?"

"Not really," she answers. She admits that her husband wanted her to stay home more in those years, although he couldn't see any way to cut back at his law firm. She felt that she had worked too hard to become a doctor to give it up. "And then I could hear the voices in my head, voices of all the men who had told me that there was no point in letting women into medical school, because they would just quit and have babies."

Even in our bleakest moments, none of us wanted to quit. Perhaps we all had blinders on. To this day we don't truly understand why people hearing our stories think that leaving medicine was a viable option, anymore than we understand why people think we could have had babies during training. It may be that some women left medical school to have children, and other women left medicine for their children. It's not that we thought about those possibilities and reasoned against them. We didn't even see them.

Patients need to believe that their doctors are in control, so they project equanimity onto us that we don't contest, even if it's false. They are often surprised to hear that we cope with the same problems they do. Most men and women have to keep their work and home lives separate to function effectively. It's not an issue that's unique to women or to doctors. It may come more easily to us, because even at work, we have to make sure that we preserve confidentiality, to prevent one visit from leaking into the next. In training, we quickly learned to spare our non-medical friends the details of our days. All of us felt this burden keenly as young mothers. Once I answered my page when I was on a play date with my older son. The office told me that one of my favorite patients had died in surgery. I didn't tell anyone what the call was about: death was not part of the daily lives of the other mothers.

Men routinely compartmentalize work and family, but because they often don't know the details of the home life, they don't have to work as hard at the separation. If you're not the one who drilled Susie on the spelling words or helped make her Halloween costume, you're not going to think about the outcome of the test the next day or regret missing the parade. In Judith's case, her husband wasn't there much of the week, to cope with their son on a day-to-day basis. Our society cuts men who are high earners a lot of slack in the fatherhood department. They are "good providers." A mother who continues to function at work while her children act out is suspect. A male science professor quoted in *Athena Unbound* says, "For a man to decide not to take his career seriously is like admitting he takes drugs. For a woman to say she puts her family ahead of career is considered a virtue; the pressures are all in that direction."

While Dan was away at school, Judith's younger son Tim prepared for his Bar Mitzvah. This was a somewhat unexpected development, since Judith is not Jewish and there hadn't been any question of Dan following his father's tradition, given his problems. But Tim seemed game, and it was important to his father. I remember Judith expressing relief that she as a non-Jew would be allowed to stand on the bimah, or platform, with Tim and Bob and his parents. The rabbi had questioned her participation.

(All of us girls have turned out to be more observant in our religious traditions than our parents were. From articles in the popular press, I have learned that my Jewish friends reflect their generation in this regard. In my case, living so close to illness and death pushed me toward some spiritual practice.)

We girls did not have a chance to speak to Judith at the temple before Tim's Bar Mitzvah ceremony began. It was a lovely June day and the large synagogue was full, with two families, because it was a double Bar Mitzvah. Apparently, we Baby Boomers are so prolific, and so many girls have Bat Mitzvahs these days, that there are not enough Saturdays to accommodate the coming of age of each Jewish child individually. Tim did a good job reading his Torah portion, and all went smoothly, until it was time for him to give his speech. Then, instead of praising his parents, and thanking them, he complained that they had forced him to undertake religious training against his will.

"Oh my God," Lorraine whispered to me, "This is supposed to be the good kid." It was as though a valedictorian had used a graduation speech to say that his parents had pushed him too hard to achieve in school. He sounded ungrateful and petulant, particularly compared to the other boy, who mouthed all the right platitudes.

Next, it was Judith and Bob's turn to say what a joy it had been to bring up their son, the one scowling at them from his seat on the bimah. Bob approached the platform and stumbled, looking faint. Judith and the rabbi grabbed him and sat him down. All the doctors in the crowd were poised to come forward, sure that Bob had suffered a heart attack after his son's speech. But Bob rallied and waved back the relatives in the front who had reached him. He and Judith gave their speeches of praise and love.

We girls learned later that Bob and Tim had been up most of the night negotiating whether Tim would go through with the ceremony. There had been calls to the rabbi after midnight and considerable tension all around. Bob had also neglected to eat breakfast. Tim sat through the rest of the service, then disappeared. He did not show up for kiddush or attend his party.

The party, catered at the UC Berkeley Faculty Club, went forward as scheduled, but despite the beautiful day and the wonderful food, the atmosphere was heavy. Judith, who had every right to hide in the bathroom and cry, as far as I was concerned, did not falter in her hostess duties. As I left, I tried to express to Judith the empathy I felt (after all, I had a thirteen-year-old of my own, and I thanked God and the Episcopal Church that we didn't have to shepherd him through a Bar Mitzvah). She explained that Tim had also given the speech at his eighth grade graduation a few days before and she thought his circuits had overloaded. Her words held compassion for her son, not anger.

Lorraine was so upset by Tim's behavior that she scheduled an appointment with her rabbi (a different one) the following week to ask how he would have coped with the situation. Given that her twins were four at the time, her concern seemed a little excessive, but she also had an adopted son who had already exhibited "issues" in preschool, and she was worried. Ruth's older son, at nine, was the next child in line for a Bar Mitzvah, but none of us were concerned about him. He was a chip off the old studious, obsessive-compulsive block.

At our parenting meeting, Judith told us that Bob's parents had sent them a letter when the boys were fourteen years old, saying that they were bad parents, that Bob was too permissive, and Judith worked too much. The rest of us were horrified.

"What did you do?" we asked with one voice.

"Well, I asked Bob if he wanted to answer it, because I sure didn't. And he said no. So I threw it away." We laughed, because we knew that the story of their boys has a happy ending. Dan returned from his expensive boarding school freed from the demons that had possessed him in middle school and attended high school at home. Everyone survived the teenage years. Both boys graduated from college this year, Dan from the University of Hawaii and Tim from Yale. I saw them recently, standing proudly by their father as he took the oath of office as a judge of the California Superior Court.

My children's issues were not as difficult as those Judith faced, although my oldest, Alan, kept us humble. He was tenacious from the beginning. I carried him well past forty weeks, despite long walks and daily swims. I never went into labor. I could feel him kick, but I dreamed that he reabsorbed back through the stages we had learned—embryo, blastocyst, blastomere—and disappeared. When I was two weeks late, I "risked out" of the alternative birth center. When I was three weeks late, my doctor put me in the hospital, broke my water, and gave me the drug Pitocin to start my labor. He says now that I must be mistaken about my dates, that they wouldn't have let me go more than two weeks, but I remember Alan's long fingernails and the concern about his blood glucose because he was postmature.

The winter Alan was born, 1981-82, was one of the rainiest on record in Northern California, and Alan was a child who never slept. Stuck indoors, I sat him in a baby seat on the kitchen counter while I baked bread and talked to him. The rain pounded on the roof of our bungalow. At night, when my husband returned from the city, I wrote *How To Survive Medical School*. I felt utterly alone. After years of moving with my husband and friends from college to medical school to residency training, of directing every waking breath toward medicine, suddenly I was on stage in a role I had barely seen and certainly had never rehearsed. By the time I was able to drive, Judith was back to work, and I knew very few other mothers.

I did try to join a mother's group in my neighborhood, but I couldn't hang. The women quoted their pediatricians, often guys I knew from training, as though each word came from a Higher Authority. Some of the women were still mourning the fact that they had Cesarean sections. Rather than taking pleasure in the child in front of them, they were planning their next perfect vaginal birth. I had a Cesarean section, too, but after all the disasters I had seen in labor and delivery and the intensive care nursery, I was grateful for a healthy baby. As a third-year student, I watched the delivery of a baby with anencephaly: no cerebral cortex, just a skull full of fluid on ultrasound. While the mother was in labor, the obstetrician inserted a needle through the cervix into the soft spot of the baby's skull to draw off some of the fluid so the head would fit through the birth canal. Once he was born, I held the baby, felt the plates of his skull shifting in my hands. We put him in an incubator in the corner and let him die.

I thought of telling them about the anencephalic baby. I wanted to *make* them feel lucky, but there was no point in giving them nightmares, so I just left the group. Listening to the concerns of those stay-at-home moms, I felt again that I belonged to a third gender, with a woman's body and a man's job. I was up against the Catch-22 of the working mother: I needed to talk to other working mothers, but none of us had time.

In retrospect, I'm pretty sure that I had postpartum depression, but there was no one around to notice. Miles was working long hours at the hospital, in a world that seemed as distant as another planet, although prior to the baby's birth I had been right there with him. My mother, who came for the birth, left after a week. All her babies had been girls, and she seemed afraid of my ten-pound boy. The girls trouped by to see the baby, but they didn't have time to hang out. I was afraid that I would not be able to get out of the house when the time came to go back to work, much less be the decisive, competent doctor I had been. If there had been something wrong with the baby, I would have known instantly. But the combination of sleep deprivation and hormonal flux and an alien body—huge dripping breasts, loose abdomen, itchy stitches—was all so strange, I had no sense of what normal could be.

By Alan's six-week checkup, I was interviewing for babysitters. Unlike Judith, I had neither the money nor the space for live-in help. And I realized, somewhat to my surprise, that I did not want certain sitters. Even if I'd had more money, the idea of a European au pair held no attraction for me. What would she know of our life? Of course, my husband reminds me that I interviewed one white woman (while Alan slept in his room) who complained about how the neighborhood had deteriorated with all these black people. She didn't recognize that I was black, and I ushered her out before she saw Alan.

I remember my first day back at work as one of the most daunting physical feats of my life, comparable to running a race. My breasts were thickly padded to prevent leaks, and I wore an elastic waist skirt to accommodate my new body. I cried in the car, but I cleaned up before I saw my first patient. I kept a glass of water on my desk, so my milk wouldn't dry up. At lunch, I pumped milk and when a patient didn't show up, I napped. By three o'clock I was overcome by waves of fatigue and longing for my child. I made it home, where the sitter handed Alan to me and the second shift began.

I called a woman doctor friend, a gynecologist, to discuss a patient a few months later. I knew she had had her first baby some weeks after I did, but she wasn't a close friend, and I didn't remember the exact date. When she answered the phone and heard my voice, she burst into tears and wailed, "It's my first day back. Does it get any easier?" Yes, I reassured her, a veteran of several months by then. The last time I had cried was at the pediatrician's. He was a grandfatherly type, near retirement (none of my peers had enough experience for me) with five children of his own. I poured out my tale of woe, my conflicts about going back to work, my concerns that Alan would be emotionally stunted for life. He let me vent, then said calmly, "Alan has a mother who's a doctor. Could be worse." I laughed and dried my tears.

My first sitter was a black woman, old enough to be my mother. I liked her well enough, but we argued over whether she should give Alan my breast milk. I nursed for nine months, pumping at work, which was a huge inconvenience. She looked at the frozen breast milk, bluish and thin compared to baby formula, and decided that the breast milk wasn't as nutritious for the baby. Of course, the opposite is true, and although I had heard patients reach the same ignorant conclusion (black women nurse less than white women, too, for many reasons, not the least being the memory of the slave wet nurse) it drove me wild as a mother and a doctor to see her set aside my milk. I made Miles talk to her because I couldn't stay rational.

We moved past the breast milk business, but when Alan started to crawl, she announced that she was too infirm to take care of a moving baby. Next came a black woman I had to fire because she simply loaded my child in the car with her and dragged him about on her errands all day. I was paying her top dollar to focus on my son, not to do her grocery shopping. When one of the doctors at work mentioned that he had met my son visiting a patient in the hospital with this sitter, I was outraged that she would casually expose him to the germs that I feared bringing home.

Then came a Latina woman, who was fine until she moved away. Finally, I gave up on a sitter in the house and starting taking Alan to the home of a Chinese woman with a little girl the same age. He was there about six months before she decided two children were too much. (My son was considerably more rambunctious than her daughter.)

At that point I had had it with individual sitters. I'd been through four and Alan had yet to turn three. Like Judith, I was the one who had to do all the hiring and firing. I was practicing full time and trying to finish my book. I desperately needed a stable childcare situation. So when I learned that the Montessori school across the park had a toddler program with extended hours and they took two year olds who were not toilet trained, I signed Alan up.

I tried to toilet train Alan, two and a half, over the summer before my second child was due, letting him run naked in our backyard. I dreaded having two children in diapers. He didn't seem to get it, and I gave up, resigned to the fact that he would regress anyway as soon as the baby was born. That's what all the books said. In fact, his teacher sent a note home while I was in the hospital after the birth, asking why I still sent him to school in diapers. I laughed with delight. As we often say of patients who report atypical symptoms, he hadn't read the book.

By the time my second son, Carl, was born, we had moved to Berkeley. The contractor who renovated our new house had a sister who was basically a stay-at-home mom, but needed extra income to pay for the mortgage on a house a few blocks from us. She was white and her husband was black. He worked as a firefighter for the city of Berkeley. She had two daughters of her own, in elementary school. I felt comfortable with Laurie immediately: I figured a woman with mixed-race children of her own would not harbor hidden prejudice.

Laurie was a Berkeley native, and her daughters attended public schools. I think she was genuinely puzzled by my life, one child in extended-day nursery school, the other in her home, me at work, not full time for a doctor, but about forty hours a week. I took one day off during the week, but I worked one weekend a month and was on call every weeknight. I was enchanted with the log she kept of her activities with Carl. She recorded their trips to the park, how long he napped, how much breast milk he drank.

There was a different work ethic in Berkeley, where adults lounged in cafes in the daytime (professors, I supposed, and writers and the many trust fund baby boomers who found the city congenial) and people pieced together several jobs to avoid the corporate grind. Mothers were different, too. When Carl turned two, Laurie started a morning playgroup for five two-year-olds instead of keeping Carl all day. Although nationally, the majority of mothers stop breastfeeding by the time their child is six months old, the four other mothers in the group were still nursing their toddlers. On my day off, when I picked Carl up, I took him home. The other mothers lifted their shirts and chatted while they nursed. I was also the only mother who hired a sitter to pick her baby up.

When Miles first started in practice, he had some slack in his schedule; one day he only did procedures, with no time in the office. (In the not-too-distant past, doctors in our community used to take an afternoon off each week to golf, or to teach.) He often was able to pick up one of the children. As his practice gained momentum, however, we found it harder to meet the six o'clock deadline at Alan's daycare. At one point, my husband said, "Hire a babysitter to pick him up." I couldn't do this. I thought ten hours without his parents was enough.

This was the moment that my career became the secondary one. The six o'clock deadline for me meant that I was not available for evening hospital consults. I was on call by beeper for my own patients, and in a true emergency I would have had to leave the kids somewhere to go in, but I was not available for routine consultation the way my colleagues were. I knew at the time that this limitation was not good for business, but I also wanted to see my children.

Cooking dinner with two needy toddlers underfoot was a nightly trial. Once again, this devolved into mostly my problem. I came home first; I started dinner. Yet the kids needed my attention. A photo from one of those evenings shows me dressed in my doctor clothes on the floor hugging Carl. It was difficult to hold them off long enough to change clothes. I put an advertisement in the UC Berkeley student newspaper for a mother's helper: "Dishes, Diapers, Dinner." After several interviews, I hired a junior from New Jersey, recently transferred from Yale, to help us from four to eight, three days a week.

Hiring Deirdre was a great move. Her father is an obstetrician, so she understood the craziness of the medical lifestyle. She was white, but living with an adopted Korean brother had opened her eyes about what it meant to be non-white. She showed us an article she had written about him, published in *Seventeen* magazine. She was bright, high-energy and flexible. She could make dinner while I played with the kids or vice versa. She was an extra pair of hands to do the dishes while I started the bath or read the first story. One of four children herself, she enjoyed sharing our family dinner, and we enjoyed hearing about her courses and meeting her beaux. Joe, the one she married, taught Alan to ride a bike after Miles and I failed. Later, they moved to Taos, New Mexico, and built a house on the mesa.

After childcare came the school decisions. I attended private schools because my parents wanted the "best" education for me, even if I was isolated from other black people. My husband attended the Hopkins School and Exeter, after public grammar school. We were members of the first Harvard class to have 10 percent black students, and racial tension was palpable during our college years.

While we are both grateful for our education, I, particularly, found the token role onerous. One medical school professor said to me that he hoped Miles and I would have children because it was important for "people like us," presumably bright, assimilated black people, to have offspring. We appeared to be poster children for affirmative action. The fact that we both came from middle-class families who had sent students to the Ivy League before affirmative action existed was lost on most people, who didn't know that there was a black middle class.

So while my girlfriends from medical school opted for private schools, I sent Alan to our neighborhood public school, where a third of the students were black. Our immediate neighborhood is largely white. Berkeley buses children from other neighborhoods to achieve racial balance. On the first day of kindergarten, a teacher tried to send Alan home on the bus, assuming he did not live nearby, and the babysitter picking him up couldn't find him. It was a close call. Fortunately, they located him on the bus before it pulled out.

Alan was young for his grade (a November birthday) and floundered socially. He complained that he was "fake black," because he didn't talk like the other black kids. After kindergarten, we moved him to one of the few private schools in the area that has ten percent blacks, and a third minority children. We bought him a peer group that included other affluent blacks. We looked at what was then considered the most prestigious school in Oakland, but we didn't apply. Alan would have been the only black child in his class, and there was no daycare, because the few mothers who worked had nannies.

When the time came for Carl to start school, we sent him to the same private school. Unfortunately, his class was weaker academically, and he always seemed to miss the good teachers. He was particularly unhappy in second grade, when he declared that the Beatrix Potter books his teacher had chosen were "for babies." The teacher invited the school principal to our end-of-the-year conference, where she told my husband and me that we had to face the fact that Carl might not be as bright as his older brother. She said that we intimidated Carl because we were high achievers.

Of course, this was nonsense (what seven year old even knows that a doctor is a "high achiever"?) It was the teacher who was intimidated by us (that's why the principal was there), but at the time, I worried that I was somehow oppressing my child with my MD. Now, I think it is a measure of the free-floating mother guilt I carried that I even paid attention to her. I turned to Carl's former nursery school teacher, a woman with five children of her own, who was my "mentor mom," and I asked her what I should do. "Send him to stay with relatives," she advised.

Third grade went better, with a new teacher whose wisecracks amused Carl. But I remembered my mentor mom's advice, and it occurred to me that it wouldn't hurt my middle child to have some quality time alone with people who adored him, even if no relatives fit the bill. So I called Deirdre in Taos, and sent Carl for two weeks to New Mexico the summer after third grade. He had a great time, and the visit became a yearly tradition. I learned only recently that he told people that he was Joe's son by another woman, and Joe played along with the joke. When the other children also showed up in subsequent summers, people were astounded. In Taos, there was no black community, and everyone who wasn't Native American and didn't speak Spanish fell into the category "Anglo." The Chinese family in town was "Anglo" and so was Carl. New Mexico gave my children a different perspective on race and ethnicity.

During my third pregnancy, I tried to learn from past experience. I closed my private practice, and imagined taking as much as four months off before I looked for a job, extra time that I coveted. (A friend hearing me daydream about those extra months said, "You know, you can take a vacation without having a child.") I hired a babysitter ahead of time. I told my obstetrician that I was not going to suffer through both labor and a Cesarean section a third time and scheduled the operation a week before my due date. My mother planned her flight for the day before.

Unfortunately, during my pregnancy, the two most important men in my life, Miles and my business partner, both herniated discs in their low back. My partner developed pain first, before Hannah was born. He took all the Tylenol with codeine from the sample drawer and lay on the floor between patient visits. After Hannah was born, my husband's pain began. He also took Tylenol with codeine, and lay on the floor at home. The children used to climb over him to hug him. My partner was desperate enough to consider surgery. I urged him to have the operation, if he was going to have one, before I left, but he hoped physical therapy would work.

A few weeks before my Cesarean date, my partner gave up and scheduled his operation, for two months later. I agreed to see his patients while he was out, since he had covered my practice when Carl was born. Hannah was born at six a.m. At seven, my mother came to see us and told me that she was returning to Chicago that day to care for my father, who had been admitted to the hospital with a stroke. The next day, the babysitter, at home with the boys, told my husband that she was leaving. In earlier years, this series of events would have certainly triggered another bout of depression. But I had learned not to look at the big picture, but to take one step at a time. At six-weeks postpartum, I was on a plane with my baby to Chicago to help my parents. And at two months I went back to work.

When Hannah was a baby, I hired a Guatemalan and then a Mexican babysitter. (After learning medical Spanish in school, I had taken Spanish in night classes at the community college because I saw many Latino patients.) These women, legal immigrants, raised Hannah along with their own children. Our Mexican-American babysitter, now a U.S. citizen and a full-time physical therapy aide at a nursing home, stayed with us until Hannah was a teenager. She has two boys, so Hannah was her only girl, too. Hannah was bilingual as a toddler, and we all absorbed the Latin culture, at least the language and the food.

My babysitters' children and my own teens attended (public) Berkeley High School together, where Carl played varsity soccer. The coach was Chicano, and more of the players spoke Spanish as their first language than English. Freshman year, the practices were mostly conducted in Spanish. All the children studied Spanish in school, and our family spent some vacations in Mexico. We wrote letters of support for citizenship and co-signed on a mortgage. Alan took two trips to Guatemala with the families of babysitters, and Hannah served as a *Dama*, or attendant, in the Quinceañera (15th birthday celebration) of another babysitter's daughter. They had met as toddlers and stayed friends in school. Speaking Spanish offers my kids another way to cope with being upper-middle-class black kids in a world where black means poor, until proven otherwise. Sometimes they let people assume they are darker-skinned Latin, rather than give a sociology lecture.

Two neighborhood groups helped me, as a working mother, form ties with families near us. We belonged to a babysitting co-op for childcare on Friday and Saturday nights. A mother I met on the playground of the local elementary school invited us to join, even though the boys were in private school. When it was our turn to host, once a month or so, it was like a birthday party from seven to ten p.m., with a dozen or more school-aged kids. We rented movies and served popcorn. I stocked and supervised an arts and crafts table. It was exhausting, but we collected enough IBM cards, our medium of exchange, to pay for several nights out ourselves. Our children wanted us to go out: Kids Co-op was more fun than hanging around with us.

Another group of neighborhood mothers and I formed a monthly mother-daughter (five of each) book group when the girls were in fourth grade, which lasted until their junior year of high school. We started with children's books, including some classics like *Heidi* and *Tom Sawyer*, and moved on to adult books as the girls matured. The one book all ten of us liked was *Bel Canto* by Ann

Patchett: we Moms identified with the hostages and the girls identified with the young guerillas.

When Alan was in sixth grade, he wrote an essay about his family. The part about me began, "My mother has a very stressful job." I was working at Kaiser by then, and barely able to cope. In junior high, he started acting out, right on schedule. He chose public high school, despite our misgivings, but then had only one word to describe his experience: "boring." He lied about doing his homework, he came home drunk, we found a joint in his pocket. I hired a math tutor for him, who told me to save my money, that Alan understood the material. For a while I had a weekly phone check-in with his math teacher to make sure the homework was getting in. Alan repeated a semester of math and did no better the second time around. He was kicked out of his private SAT preparation class for coming late and disrupting the class. When we tried to ground him, he left and didn't return all night.

In the middle of Alan's junior year of high school, when he was flunking math and his friends were stealing money from us, I wrote in my journal, "I feel that I have passed through anger with Alan and come out the other side to a resigned sadness." Then, "Every time I think about him I cry. So I try not to think about him." Fortunately, he matured right on schedule also, and pulled good enough grades in his other subjects to meet the required average for the University of California.

Like Judith's children, mine have floated to calmer seas. The younger ones made a greater intellectual investment in high school and reaped the benefit. Alan graduated from U.C. Santa Cruz, where he never had to take a math course. Carl is a senior at Columbia University and Hannah is at Brown University. They can all speak standard English, black English, or Spanish, as the occasion requires.

9. More Families

"Women are a widely accepted part of the medical community. But in this field as in many others, the most intense social pressures around femininity are now shifted to a later phase of women's lives—when they have families." (Anna Fels, *Necessary Dreams*, 2004)

Ruth was running late, headed for an assembly she'd promised to attend at her son Jake's school. Nothing is harder than slipping out of the office in the middle of the day. Since this was Jake's first year in school, she wasn't used to this kind of obligation, and she was vaguely annoyed that it seemed like such a big deal. It was only kindergarten, after all. Her husband David worked forty minutes away, at Kaiser, where the schedules were less flexible. He couldn't make it. Dressed in her operating room scrubs, she dashed out, jumped into the car and faced the cross-town traffic. Luckily, San Francisco is small. Nothing is far, if there's a parking space. She sprinted for the auditorium and slid into the seat her babysitter had saved for her.

The babysitter handed over Peter, her younger boy, who was two and squirmy. Just as Ruth was about to get up and leave to take Peter out, Jake stood up by himself onstage. In a clear, sweet, high-pitched voice he sang a solo in a Native American language. He had practiced in secret, so Ruth had no idea what was coming. "I sat there with tears streaming down my face. I looked over at my friend Sue, another GI doctor mom, and she was crying, too. I felt like she was the only other person in the room who had struggled as much as I had to get there." Since then, Jake has toured the world with his college a cappella group—Judith and I heard them sing when they were in town last year—and he has shown an amazing facility with languages. It was all there, that day.

Ruth and Karen had their children after Judith and I became mothers, and they made opposite lifestyle choices. Ruth focused more on career and Karen more on family. Karen had three girls, the last born when she was forty. Ruth started about the same time, in her mid thirties, but stopped at two boys.

Ruth repeats the word "clueless" to describe her debut as a mother. She marvels that she was unaware of the linear decline in a woman's fertility after age thirty. She assumed that when the time came that she'd be able to get pregnant, "and luckily it worked out." The year Judith and I had our first children, Ruth had an abortion, because she still had years of training ahead. Like all of us, Ruth and Karen had their first babies the moment they were married and out of training.

The first postpartum days were rocky. Ruth's mother left the day after Ruth came home from the hospital. "I was angry, and it brought up a lot of old stuff, how she was never there for me." Those of us who didn't have warm and fuzzy mothers still hope that they will turn into warm and fuzzy grandmothers. When David went back to work after a week, Ruth felt she couldn't cope. She was very anemic, and the fatigue was "worse than anything I could have imagined." Coming from a woman who spent every third or fourth night on call as an intern and resident, that's saying a lot. She had hired a nanny, but that woman was not available for two weeks. So she hired an "old-time baby nurse" to help her in the interim. The help allowed Ruth to get more sleep, take her iron, and drink fluids for breastfeeding. She nursed each boy for the three months until she went back to work, when her milk "evaporated under the stress."

Ruth struck gold with her first nanny, a young English woman. She lived with the family for a year. When she married, she moved out, but continued to work with the boys until she had her first child. Then her sister took over. The sister stayed with the family for fourteen years. Ruth describes the first sister as gentle and competent. "I would do anything to keep her. I paid for her car, I gave her raises."

The second sister was fine when the children were young, but eventually Ruth had some reservations about her child rearing philosophy. A friend told her about an incident when the nanny came to pick up Peter and berated him for being too slow. The friend described Peter as "white as a sheet" under the verbal assault. The boys never complained, but Ruth wonders now if they were protecting her, knowing how stressed she was. She feels guilty, that she may have missed other clues that all was not well. Lately she has learned that the nanny told the boys, "Your parents don't set any limits." It may be inevitable that the person who spends the day with the children will see them in a different light than the parents who feel they only have a few hours to cherish them, but we all felt that since we were paying top dollar for childcare, the nannies should respect our rules, about breast milk or behavior.

Before the children were born, Ruth and David threw a meal together some-how, late at night. (Ruth does not cook. Once, when Miles and I came to dinner, she had to ask her older son how to turn on the new oven.) With the boys, they needed a more organized, earlier mealtime, so they started using a take-out food service. Eventually, they hired a second full-time employee, who served as a housekeeper and cooked dinner. She worked from twelve to eight. With a second employee, the nanny could get home to her own family at a reasonable time, and Ruth's husband, who relieved the babysitter, had more flexibility.

Once Ruth went into private practice, shortly after her second son was born, she began to work the twelve-hour days that are still the norm for her. David has a longer commute, but he does not have to consult on new patients in the hospital after his office hours. Ruth felt that she could never turn down a request to see a patient, because that doctor might not refer to her again. Under the Kaiser system, where referrals are locked in to the few gastroenterologists at each facility, only the person on call for the hospital would have to see a patient after office hours, and then only emergency cases.

In his younger days, David was a rock climber and skier, out of doors as much as he could be. By the time the children were born, he had ten years of practicing behind him, and knee arthritis was starting to slow him down on the slopes. He was happy to invest his extra energy in his boys. With some regret, Ruth describes her husband as the "primary parent" for her second son. "It was so much work to build a practice, I had to be so available, that I never bonded with Peter the way I did with Jake."

In addition to the time constraints, there was a difference in temperament between the two boys. Peter is a jock like his father. They are great companions now, watching football games together on TV. Jake tried sports when he was little, for his father's sake, but was relieved to relinquish that role to Peter when he showed more natural talent in that direction. Jake is the quiet scholar.

Although Ruth's sons both excelled in school, even Ruth had to face a more casual attitude toward academics with her second son. She tells a story of the family sitting around the dinner table, discussing whether he needed to do the extra credit work assigned. "There we were, three people [she, her husband, and their older son] who had never in our lives considered not doing all the extra credit work assigned, listening to this boy, who protested that the teacher shouldn't have called it extra credit if she wanted everyone to do it. And we had to admit, he was right."

A friend at Kaiser once described his practice as a "General Motors practice." Ruth has a Cadillac practice. Her patients are wealthy and socially prominent in

San Francisco. Her children have attended the most prestigious private schools in the city. "Every time I go to a school function, fifteen patients mob me and tell everybody how wonderful I am. I think the boys like the fact that I am so well known in this community." Most of the other mothers at her children's school don't work. In fact, Ruth says that many of them are the second wives of older men. Ruth receives considerable recognition as a doctor, but she feels isolated as a mother pursuing a career. We all have ambivalence about the values of women in high society, the culture of shopping and liposuction.

In San Francisco, the cost of living is so high that many families flee to other communities. Ruth and David decided to stick it out in the city, but it meant that Ruth, the higher earner, assumed a greater financial burden than the rest of us, to pay for the two full-time employees and the private schools that allowed her to work so hard. As her older son heads off to college, she speaks more of the trade-off she made to find success along the traditional path for male doctors. Although Ruth says that her closest friends are other mothers, she did not have much time for friendship. She didn't have time for anything except work and the kids. "We used to have a subscription to the symphony, but we let it lapse, because we never made it." Even in her profession, she has not found time for the kind of unpaid activity that can add variety to a life in practice, like a political role in a professional group or the clinical teaching Judith and I have enjoyed. Ruth stopped teaching at the medical center when the children were young and never went back.

What I noticed in the early days, when we dragged our children with us to our meetings, is that Ruth seemed tentative with the boys, anxious about doing the right thing. She was nervous from the beginning, and there is no clear path to being a good mother, much less the best. As someone who had checked out all the books in the library about children's games before each birthday party, I recognized the symptoms, but I learned early on to trust my children's amazing capacity to love me despite my ineptitude. Ruth, blessed with stable childcare, worried at a deeper level: she was afraid that her children wouldn't be able to tell who was the nanny and who was the mom.

It is hard for me to imagine the kind of grim intellectual fidelity to the profession Ruth takes for granted. When we get together, I feel like an intellectual floozy in the presence of her monastic dedication to medicine. Yet there was a time when even Ruth, our soldier, almost lost it. Depression stalked her as well.

One day, when Jake and Peter were nine and five, Ruth entered her exam room in her office and greeted one of her regular patients, a psychologist. The psychologist took one look at her and said, "I can't let you keep doing this to yourself."

At first Ruth tried to pretend that allergies made her eyes puffy, not crying in the bathroom between patients. She didn't want to admit that she had gained fifty pounds. But she accepted the referral the psychologist made and started therapy again for the first time since training.

Years later, in my living room, I ask her what exactly was the problem.

"I think it was just the cumulative stress, at home and at work. I always felt guilty about the children and I always felt that I had to be the best of the best at work."

"What did David say about your patient's intervention?"

She laughs. "Oh, he was relieved. He had already thrown out all the pills in the house so I wouldn't take them." David had tried to help her, but she had ignored him. For some of us, it takes an outsider to say, "Enough. You don't have to prove anything anymore."

When we heard this story, the rest of us remembered the time when Ruth had put on weight, but we had not figured out how depressed she had become. This is partly because we saw each other only a few times a year in those days, but also because we were all under relentless pressure. At that time Judith and I were coping with our teenagers and Lorraine had preschool twins. Our lives were bound by work, the children, and the children's activities. Ruth's deeper angst did not stand out against the background of our chronic stress.

Ruth's boys sailed through their Bar Mitzvahs, held at a historic temple in San Francisco. My mind always wanders during the long passages of Hebrew, often back to the first Bar Mitzvah I attended at age thirteen, for one of my classmates. Then, as a child myself, I was awed by my classmate. Now, I feel the collective pride. Sitting next to me, as Jake sang his Torah portion, Lorraine pointed out, not for the first time, how proud Ruth's husband always seems of her, too.

Ruth is looking much more relaxed these days, now that her boys are both at Harvard. Even better, before he left for college, her older son laid into her about her parenting. She beamed when she told us what he yelled at her: "You're so over involved with me." She's done her bit to uphold the stereotype of the Jewish mother, despite working sixty hours a week.

In Karen's case, it was her later marriage, not further training, that delayed her childbearing. We had wondered whether having stepchildren might discourage Karen from having her own, but (as she says) walking into a family of teenagers bears no relationship to having a baby. The older children lived with her husband's ex-wife and visited on alternate weekends.

Karen rearranged her practice life when her first child was born. She saw only a few patients at a time, so that she could come home to nurse, rather than pump breast milk the way I did, or give up nursing, as Ruth had. In later years, it would have been more efficient to cluster the patients on a few days each week, but she valued the daily balance of work and home. The downside to this system was that it increased the number of transitions between her two roles, which are the toughest times. She remembers a day when she had to get her oldest daughter home in order to go to work, but her daughter, a four year old, refused to fasten her seatbelt. After arguing a few minutes, Karen decided to drive the three blocks with her daughter unrestrained in the back seat. She knew it wasn't much of a risk, but she still felt like a bad mom, putting her child at any risk.

Karen's schedule allowed her time to work, time to be with the children, and time to have a life. Both she and her husband worked part time, and they had live-in help. When she first moved into the community, and met somewhat older mothers when she picked up her stepchildren at school, she had the impression that most of them stayed home. Now she feels that there has been a generational change, and that more of the mothers in her community are in the work force. One of her closest friends, and tennis partner, is a radiologist and mother of five who works from home, a choice made possible by new technology. The hospital sends digital x-rays to her home computer, and she sends back her reports.

Six weeks after Karen gave birth to her second child, her sixteen-year-old step-daughter left her mother's household and came to live with her father and Karen. It was a difficult time for everyone. Although the stepdaughter, Rachel, had been unhappy in her mother's house, she felt disloyal for leaving. Karen remembers that Rachel kept her up at night complaining about life, as teenagers do, when Karen, a new mom, craved sleep. "As a stepmother, I felt that I didn't have much control over how the children were raised, but I had to deal with the consequences." To some extent, all of the stepchildren were jealous of their father's new family, born when he had more time and money. When they had been young, their father was busy establishing the dental clinics that provided the income for his second family.

Karen estimates that it took about a year for everyone to get used to each other. But after the transition, she and Rachel developed a close relationship. Rachel was always a good student, and she has become a dentist like her father. When Rachel was in dental school, Karen could offer her a woman's perspective on training in a male profession, to supplement her father's advice. Rachel and her orthodontist husband now have two children. When their first child was born, Rachel lived only ten minutes away from Karen, who enjoyed helping out.

The experience reminded Karen what an identity crisis motherhood precipitates for a professional woman. "I feel lucky that I had a practice to return to right away. Rachel moved here while she was pregnant, so she had to go out and look for a job, which takes energy you don't have when you're nursing."

All of Karen's children attended the same K-12 private school that her step-children had attended before them. But Karen's oldest daughter finished at a public high school that she chose because of her interest in drama. Since junior high school, she has declined to follow the program her parents laid out. She decided that she didn't want to undertake the preparation necessary for a Bat Mitzvah in their home congregation: she wanted to skip the ritual all together. Her parents came up with a creative compromise, a Bat Mitzvah trip to Israel with a half dozen other children. There she read a shorter Torah portion at a historic mountain site. When they came home, the family hosted an outdoor party for her friends.

Karen's younger girls both had their Bat Mitzvahs at the home synagogue, the same one her husband Frank attended before they were married. He was the more observant Jew when they met and helped bring Karen to Judaism again. Frank's parents were Holocaust survivors and Frank was born in a relocation camp. His first language was Yiddish. Karen had her own Bat Mitzvah at the synagogue in 1999, joining a girlfriend who had decided to have an adult ceremony. Karen also started singing in the temple choir, which performs several times a year.

When we were young, it was unusual for a girl to have a Bat Mitzvah. None of the Jewish women in the group had one. Its popularity today reflects the influence of the feminist movement on Judaism. In the Bay Area, Lorraine, whose mother-in-law is also a Holocaust survivor, serves on the board of her temple. She recently participated in the search for a new rabbi. The board chose a woman. Lorraine and Karen have changed, but so has Judaism.

Karen now has three grandchildren (her other stepdaughter is also a mom), and one daughter left at home. Her oldest daughter, now at the University of Southern California, has turned away from the theatre and is working on the prerequisites for physical therapy school. Her younger sister, who started at Tufts this fall, has expressed an interest in psychology. "I talked to her about considering psychiatry, too, but I don't want to pressure her," Karen said to me. I feel the same way about my daughter, who is taking chemistry and math in college, and just committed to premed. Of our children, so far only she and Jake, Ruth's son, have pursued a premed path.

Lorraine's twins, adopted at birth, are three years younger than Karen's oldest child. Lorraine spent her first week of motherhood far from home, tending her babies in the living room of a small house on the East Coast. She and her husband borrowed the house from her husband's cousin who was off visiting other relatives. Otherwise they would have been stuck in a hotel room while the adoption paperwork was processed. The twins' birthday is close enough to the Fourth of July holiday that the mandatory seventy-two-hour waiting period before the birth parents could sign the final papers stretched into a week of bureaucratic delay. Nevertheless, Lorraine smiles as she remembers their makeshift nursery, two portable cribs, diapers, receiving blankets, all from Babies-R-Us at the local mall. It was a crazy, sleepless time, but Lorraine points out that the advantage of twins was that her husband was drawn into childcare from the moment of birth. "It was clear that there was no way that I could handle both of them on my own."

Toward the end of the week, Lorraine's parents-in-law showed up to help, and bundled them onto the plane when it was time to go home. Once aloft, the flight attendant announced their good news, and they received a round of applause. That was another advantage of adopting twins: it was unusual, heroic even. People who couldn't care less about children were impressed.

We girls were a little worried about how this twin business would work out. Judith had close to a twin experience, and we remembered how hard it had been. But Lorraine and her husband Sam plunged into childrearing at age forty with the same determination that had seen them through medical school. The organizational skills that served them well as doctors kept the household on an even keel, and they used all the resources at their disposal, from hired help to twin support groups. A few houses down, another doctor's wife gave birth to twins the same year, and it seemed like a twin world on that block.

Lorraine joined the faculty at UCSF that same year. Accustomed to the Kaiser model of accrued leave, she did not expect to receive maternity leave so soon. But the decision was up to the discretion of the chief who had recruited her, and he offered her three months off with pay. She has the distinction of being the only one of us who enjoyed a fully paid maternity leave. Even when she returned to work, since she was new, her clinic practice was not as busy as it would become, and she could work three days a week.

The contrast with Ruth, who also changed jobs within a year of childbirth, but went into private practice, is striking. Lorraine, salaried, could afford to direct her time toward her children. Ruth had to borrow from her husband's retirement fund to pay the overhead in her new office. She also had a relatively light appointment schedule at first, but she used the extra time to schmooze doctors at the hospital for referrals rather than to return to her son.

Like Ruth, Lorraine had good luck with childcare from the start. The first babysitter she hired stayed with the family for four and a half years. Lorraine says that she paid more than anyone she knew for a babysitter, partly because she had twins, partly because she wanted to keep her. Lorraine's nanny was somewhat older than the women Ruth and Judith had hired, and did not live in. Lorraine wrote up a weekly menu, and she, Sam, and the nanny all contributed to the dinner effort, depending on who was most available on any given day.

Lorraine and her husband had only been married a few years before the adoption, and they were both climbing the academic ladder later than usual, Lorraine because she had spent the years at Kaiser, Sam because he had started medical school at an older age. Although they were at different hospitals in very different specialties, the academic hierarchy is so well defined—assistant professor, associate professor, tenured professor—that it was easy for them to compare their progress. Of the two doctor couples in our group, they competed the most directly. Once their careers took off, it was difficult for either one of them to cut back, and Lorraine, who performed laser surgery, was the higher earner. She feels that she has struggled hard to maintain a balance between home and career. She has always worked from home one day a week, for instance. But Sam accused her of making her career the priority.

One of the practical ways the competition impacted family life was the issue of business travel. Academic doctors travel for work much more than other doctors, giving lectures at conferences and universities. As Lorraine's stature in pediatric dermatology rose, she was asked to speak all over the world. She turned down many invitations, but Sam complained that she was always away. When the twins were young, the childcare burden for the parent at home was intense. Most people dread long plane flights, but for Lorraine, the hours in transit (business class) were rare moments of solitude, a guilty pleasure. Sam and Lorraine both enjoyed the Premier Executive perks that they earned with frequent flyer miles, and the miles became another symbol of success. If one of them fell below the threshold number for Premier Executive status, it was a big deal. It seemed that their lives were one long negotiation, over travel, over childcare, with both of them feeling they had to compromise too much. Then fate intervened.

In 2000, Sam was diagnosed with Hodgkin's lymphoma, a cancer of the lymphatic system. He had chemotherapy and radiation, and he has passed the five years that define a cure. During his treatment, Lorraine cancelled everything she could, curtailed her traveling, and called on relatives to be with Sam when his treatment conflicted with her work obligations. But she continued to work, partly because work was a solace to her, but also, if God forbid, Sam didn't make it, she would be the sole wage earner. "Sometimes that's what scares me the most," she told me then. "I lost my parents young. I lived through it. But I don't know how I would cope with the kids alone." She tried to keep the household routine as close to normal as possible for the twins, who were in fifth grade at the time. It was her responsibility, and she approached it as another job. The transportation logistics alone, when her husband was going back and forth for treatments and too weak to drive, required higher math skills.

Sam still has some mild physical problems, like neuropathy from the chemotherapy. But the biggest difference is psychological. Having a life-threatening disease made him think about some things, other than work, that he'd like to do before he dies. Always an avid biker, he bought a road bike and trained for a century ride. He has taken up swimming and started to write. Whether it was the kids growing older, or the whole family having to pull together during the stress of Sam's illness, or Sam and Lorraine's evolution as a couple, the tension over work and childcare responsibilities dissipated.

Lorraine's twins, a boy and a girl, look nothing alike. Todd is a muscular blonde boy, a solid presence. His sister Susan is a dark-haired slip of a girl. As soon as they started preschool, it became clear that their strengths and weaknesses are also in different areas. Susan is a social butterfly, who struggles with academics. Todd, who could tell time before his fourth birthday and was reading in kindergarten, does not make friends easily. Lorraine, as a pediatrician, recognized that Todd had a slight speech impediment at age three, because his speech was still not intelligible to adults outside the family. A year of speech therapy took care of that, but at age four, the director of the nursery school suggested that they send him for psychological therapy. He did not play well with others, and occasionally hit his classmates when he was frustrated. Much to Lorraine's chagrin as a dermatologist, he also pulled out his hair when he was anxious. It wasn't unheard of behavior for a preschool-aged boy, but the director was concerned. By age six, Todd was a veteran of both speech and psychological therapy, and Lorraine had engaged the first of many tutors to help Susan with reading.

The private school the children attended when they were little was one that made accommodations for children with issues. It also ran on a year-round schedule, which was a great attraction for working mothers. At parent meetings, Lorraine did not have to cope with the Armani and Gucci scene that Ruth faced. But Ruth never had to worry about her children's behavior or grades the way Lorraine did. Although Ruth puts in as many hours as Lorraine, she still says her closest friends are other mothers. In contrast, Lorraine finds more support from colleagues at work. Lorraine also commutes across the bay to her job, so there is literal and psychological distance between her work world and her family. When she walks into her children's school, no one knows she is a doctor unless she tells them.

As a biological parent, I believed in my older son's intellectual capacity, but I oscillated between good mom and bad mom. Good mom was engaged and kept up with his assignments, hired the math tutor, asked to read his essays. Bad mom left him alone, because nobody helped me through high school. And I was so tired at night. Lorraine has the same struggle, times two, with her children. She doesn't want to pressure Susan to do work that is beyond her or lean on Todd to be Mr. Congeniality. On the other hand, she wants to help them realize their full potential. She worries that not sharing the same genes puts her at a disadvantage in understanding them, that the adoption is like a gauzy curtain that prevents her from truly seeing them. And she is so tired at night.

The twins are starting their senior year of high school. Both of her children attend competitive private high schools, an outcome that was not at all clear when they were in first grade. Their combined Bar and Bat Mitvah went off without a hitch, proving either that Lorraine's years of worry paid off, or that she didn't need to worry. Lorraine says that she wishes she were as successful a parent as she is a dermatologist. She says that other people have complimented her on how involved she is with her children, despite her high-powered job, but she doesn't see it.

I would say, that is the problem, that she doesn't see. At work, Lorraine is at the top of a rigid hierarchy in a subspecialty. She is accustomed to the kind of mastery and control that Judith and I, slogging along in general medicine, coaxing patients into lifestyle changes and never knowing what kind of problem will walk in the door, can only dream about. Parenting is not an arena where mastery and control have any meaning.

In our careers, we fought against society's expectations of the role of women in the workplace. Then, when we became mothers, society said that we put our children at risk. All of us felt vulnerable to this accusation. What could we say? Once again, the change in the political climate worked against us. The backlash to feminism caught us in the face. With a huge sigh of relief, I report that the bottom line is that our children have flourished.

When I look back at how we coped as mothers, I am impressed with the variety of ways we found. In every couple, the higher earner ended up with the stronger career, which I doubt is accidental. Otherwise, we went with what worked for us. It is hard for many women to accept that there is no "right" way to mother. Public school moms denounced me when I sent my kids to private schools, and private school moms told me how dangerous Berkeley High was. Our medical training taught us to be less judgmental, to respect other people's choices. Our children have mothers who are doctors. Could be worse.

Lorraine recently worked with a younger doctor, a man, whose mother is an anesthesiologist in Canada. One year, the staff celebrated Lorraine's birthday with a cake, and the younger doctor urged her to take the leftover cake home to her children. "That's what my mother used to do, when there was a party for her at work. She would bring home some cake and say, 'See? There are people who like me, who think I am a good person!'" He laughed, Lorraine laughed, I laughed hearing the story later. It is a relief not to have to pretend at work that our children don't matter. The younger doctor doesn't know Lorraine well enough to know the particulars of her family. But he knows and respects her dual role, well enough to tease her in a loving way.

10. Second Acts

"Give the patient what he wants when he wants it"
(Kaiser slogan in the 1990s)

At the beginning of 1989, Lorraine and Ruth left the Permanente Medical Group (Kaiser), and I signed on. I started out seeing only urgent care, or same day appointment patients. Later I took on a practice, but like everyone else, I still saw a few urgent care patients. One day, my 4:15 urgent care patient was a seventy-year-old on narcotics for cancer pain who was very constipated. She presented to the emergency room, but they triaged her to the clinic for disimpaction. We had no nurses, and the procedure room in our unit did not have a bathroom, but no matter.

I evaluated the patient briefly, confirmed with a rectal exam that she was impacted and sent her to the procedure room where the medical assistant (six months training after high school) administered an enema. Then the MA left, because it was 4:30. When the medical group lost money, medical assistants were instructed not to work overtime. They worked for Kaiser Health and Hospitals, not Permanente. "We don't work for the doctors," was the answer to most requests for help. I had learned not to ask.

Fortunately, the patient was spry, because she managed to get to the bathroom down the hall herself, while I started with my 4:30 patient. When I slipped out to check on her, I found her on her way back, almost naked in the hallway, the gown falling off her. There were patients going in and out of exam rooms of other doctors, but she was so desperate for relief, she had lost all modesty.

Back in the procedure room, I checked her rectum again, because she felt that she had not fully evacuated. She was right. I tried to break up the hard stool and she hustled off to the bathroom again. I returned to the exam room with the 4:30 patient. I had a 4:45 patient to see, too, so I ran between the procedure room and the exam rooms every few minutes, gloving, ungloving, holding the patient's gown around her. Once upon a time, I was taught that my goal should be to treat every patient as though she were my mother. At Kaiser, I did the best I could, given the constraints of the system.

When I started at Kaiser, Lorraine warned me, "Don't get involved. The quicker you get involved, the quicker you'll want to leave." Initially, I signed on as a pool physician, working a few shifts a week. I saw a patient every fifteen minutes, with no chart and no expectation of a chart: medical records was so slow that they didn't try to retrieve charts even when the appointment was made several hours in advance. About 1990, they installed computers in the exam rooms, so that we could pull up the patient's medication list and their problem list (other records came online later) which was a big help. I had thought of urgent care as sore throats and sprained ankles, but I was mistaken. The first week, a man with shoulder pain turned out to have lung cancer.

Later, I saw a kidney transplant patient without a regular doctor, who explained to me he didn't want one. His previous regular doctor, a kidney specialist, didn't return the patient's phone calls for several hours and tried to handle problems over the phone. Or he might fit him in the next day. Without a regular doctor, the patient could get an urgent care appointment right away. This strategy for working the system assumed that all of us in urgent care were as qualified to treat someone with a transplant as a kidney specialist would be, which I doubted. But the patient had tried it both ways, and would not be dissuaded. I began to recognize other patients with chronic illness who valued convenience over expertise.

After a few months as a pool physician, with changing hours every week, I committed to working in urgent care the same three days each week, so they could count on me. In return, I received health benefits and some retirement benefits. I could not become a partner, and receive the bonuses and raises they did, and I could not have my own practice, but I was satisfied with this daytime Mommy track. My kids were two, five and eight. My husband's practice was busy. It turned out that I was good at making quick decisions with inadequate information, and I liked the anonymous Lone Ranger role after the years of long-term relationships in private practice.

I helped people get what they needed in the system. If I diagnosed someone with diabetes, I plugged them into the diabetes class in health education and made sure they were wait-listed for a regular doctor, in addition to starting medication. I learned to schedule them to see me in follow up because the usual wait for a regular doctor appointment was two months. Otherwise, they saw different people in urgent care, because they were too anxious to wait. There was no way to speed up the regular doctor appointment because the condition was not life-threatening (true). I felt stuck in the middle between "evidence-based" policies (a study wouldn't show any lasting difference in outcome from waiting two months for their next appointment and seeing me in two weeks) and the psychological impact of diseases on real people.

Even a sprained ankle in a 45-year-old man is more than a stretched ligament. At that age, people see a minor athletic injury as a portent. It means their body is "falling apart", that they are getting old, and doomed to decrepitude. They don't express these fears, of course. They just keep coming back because the ankle doesn't feel "quite right." I declare with confidence at the first visit that the ankle will heal, although it might heal more slowly than when they were twenty, and that they have many vital years ahead of them. I emphasize the importance of continued activity and of listening to their body more closely to avoid further injury. I talk about Jerry Rice and any other older athlete in the news. Ace-wrap, crutches and out the door is quicker initially, but not in the long run.

During this period, I studied for and passed the Geriatrics Boards. The first few geriatrics fellowships were just getting off the ground when I finished my residency and I was sick of training at that point. When they created the specialty boards, in 1990, they allowed those of us who had extensive experience working with older patients in practice to grandfather into the specialty by taking an examination. I sat for the exam in 1992, and received my certificate for "Added Qualifications in Geriatrics."

Geriatrics remains a largely academic specialty, because it's one of the few areas where the extra training leads to a lower income in private practice. Geriatric patients are slow and complex and insurance reimbursement is the same for a general internist and a geriatrician. Geriatric training is a disadvantage at Kaiser as well, because an internist's salary doesn't change if she sees a larger proportion of older patients. On the other hand, at Oakland, there was a geriatric clinic as part of the internal medicine residency training program, and it was fun to teach there one afternoon a month, in rotation with the other geriatricians. The doctors worked with a social worker, a dietician, a pharmacist, a physical therapist and an occupational therapist to do a detailed geriatric assessment.

These were also the years that I began writing again. I wrote a first person essay that I sent to the East Bay *Express* newspaper. When the editor called to say that he planned to publish it, and I told him that I was a doctor, he suggested that I contribute medical essays to the paper. I did that, two or three a year, for about ten years, until the paper's new owners decided to go in another direction.

I wrote about strep throat, head lice, hepatitis C, AIDS, menopause, cholesterol, Cesarean sections, race, old age ... almost always inspired by my patient's questions. I learned that I make sense of the world by writing about it. At my pre-employment interview at Kaiser, I mentioned that I wrote occasionally for a newspaper. The chief of medicine told me that if I were hired, I would have to run any articles past her for her approval. Fortunately, for once in my life, I didn't argue, I just ignored her. She didn't ask further, and I didn't tell.

As the people at Kaiser got to know me, they started using me as an in-house locum tenens substitute for doctors who were ill or on leave. I substituted for a gay rheumatologist who died of AIDS (most of his patients had HIV), a general internist who died of kidney failure, a nephrologist on leave for breast cancer treatment and the internist who served as the liason for the substance abuse treatment program on maternity leave. The internists in the back clinic also trained me to treat their overflow patients.

These assignments stretched me, because I was always working at the limits of my expertise. I made close friends with an advice nurse who helped me with the HIV practice. Most of the guys knew that their doctor was dying of the same disease and were not thrilled to have their care handed over to some new doctor, particularly a woman. My RN friend shared their affection for their doctor (whom I only met once) and helped them (and me) cope with the change.

It sounds like a weird way to practice but it suited me.

One day, the new chief of medicine called me in and announced that the Permanente Group had decided to eliminate the associate position. I would either have to return to the part time physician pool, with no guarantee of regular work, or go on the partnership track. There were three of us at the facility, all women with young children, who faced this choice. None of us could afford to work only occasionally, but we were all reluctant to take a practice again. We would have to work in the hospital, take night call and most onerous, shoulder the responsibility for a panel of patients. All those phone calls.

At the same time, we recognized that the fact that the Permanente Medical Group would allow us to work toward partnership on a part time basis was a huge victory for women doctors, who had lobbied hard for this concession. A woman who was part of this effort recently told me that the women felt that a part time partnership track was more important than maternity leave, so they chose to focus on the bigger issue. One reason that they were successful was that doctors near retirement age, mostly men, also wanted to work less and remain voting partners. My friend stayed on with the Permanente Group, and says ruefully, "We still don't have maternity leave."

The choice came at a particularly bad time for my family, because my husband had recently taken a 25% pay cut. His office manager blamed the decrease income on managed care. We later learned that revenues were down because of embezzlement, but at the time, I didn't know whether his salary would continue to fall. Although I had no interest in taking a practice again, I told the chief that I would.

In early 1994, Lorraine mentioned to me during our weekly walk that the woman with whom I shared an office, another associate forced to choose partnership, did not have to work in the hospital although she was on the partnership track.

I was stunned. By this time I had already added hospital duties to my schedule, and had survived a few nights of in-house hospital call supervising the residents. As night attending physicians, we only saw the patients admitted overnight to the intensive care units because the daytime attendings saw the patients admitted to the regular ward, but the first night I had ten admissions to the ICUs. (We also served as daytime attendings one month a year.)

"Yeah, she's helping the chief with her practice or something. Maybe she's ashamed to tell you."

I knew the chief was a friend of my officemate, so I called one of the assistant chiefs first, to figure out whether I was the last to know. I told her what I had heard. She was as surprised as I was.

"That can't be true. It would be so divisive."

But of course it was true. My officemate had cut a sweetheart deal with the chief, who came to talk to me about it after clinic that afternoon. She said of my officemate, "I thought you liked her." Sure I liked her. But I didn't like her enough to work more for the same pay. I didn't like anyone that much. She said that my officemate was stressed with her three children, a few years younger than mine.

I felt like screaming, "Lady, you have no idea of the stress I have." If I could have quit then and there, I would have. I wrote in my journal, "It will never be the same. Not that I truly entertained illusions of 'visible fairness.' But I want out." "Visible fairness" was part of the jargon they threw around in the Permanente Medical Group when they talked about important principles of compensation.

The rest of my time with the Permanente Group, three more years, was an act of will. I continued to share an office with the same woman. We were cordial. We both made partner, as Ruth and Lorraine had. Seeking a way to sustain my interest in the job, I applied for and to my surprise, was appointed physician Chief of Health Education. I worked with a health educator director to run the department of eight educators. It was a wonderful world, with kind people. At the beginning of meetings they did a "check in", where they went around the table and asked how everyone was feeling. I wondered whether this happened because the department was mostly women or because they were health educators. At any rate, the departmental culture was completely different from that of medicine.

Unfortunately, because of the financial panic, we couldn't focus on health education. The regional Health Education Department wanted us to support the "roll-out" of regional call centers, where medical assistants, working from algorithms, took the place of the RNs who used to answer the phones. Each station used to have a couple of advice nurses, so we doctors could poke our head in and say, "If Mrs. Jones calls again, her x-ray is scheduled for Monday." The nurse understood what the test was and could talk to the patient about it. Under the new system, the medical assistants were collected in one suburban location elsewhere, and faxed us messages. Even when the fax machine didn't jam, which was daily, none of the thirty medical assistants at the remote location knew us, or the patients.

Anxious patients who called over and over would get different MAs each time, who forwarded each message. Call backs were supposed to go through the medical assistants at our station, who also had the responsibility of putting patients in the room. The upshot was angry patients on the phone, who couldn't understand the response from the medical assistant and angry patients on site, who were kept waiting. Some of my elderly and Spanish-speaking patients started showing up at the station because they couldn't work the new phone system at all.

We doctors ended up doing almost all of our own callbacks, adding hours to our day, at lunch time and after hours. Since they had to pay the medical assistants overtime, but not the physicians, one colleague joked, in the jargon of the time, that the administration was using the physicians to leverage the time of the medical assistants. As Chief of Health Education at Oakland, I was supposed to be a "champion of the regional initiative at the Oakland health center". No way.

I faced ethical issues in health education, too. In our Oakland facility, which served a population that seemed at least half black (they didn't keep statistics on race) none of the health educators were black. There was one black educator at a Sacramento facility, but that was it for Northern California, about twenty medical centers. At a regional meeting to set practice guidelines for cancer screening I was the only person of color, because the guy from Sacramento didn't show. The PSA blood test for prostate cancer, always controversial, was the topic of discussion. The national urologist groups (prostate surgeons, not a disinterested group) advocated an annual test for all men between fifty and seventy-five. The U.S. Preventive Health Task Force said there wasn't enough evidence. I knew that outside of Kaiser, doctors were ordering the test routinely, partly for medical-legal reasons. Juries have made very clear that they don't care whether the science behind a test is solid. If guys are being tested for cancer, and Joe didn't get a test for cancer, and Joe gets cancer, the doctor is to blame.

As it happens, black men have more prostate cancer than white men, and black men in Alameda County, California have the highest rate of prostate cancer in the country. Oakland is in Alameda County. At the Oakland facility, we saw basically two groups of patients: highly educated, typically white people, many of them U.C. Berkeley employees, and working class people, often minorities, under union contracts. The affluent patients read the New York Times and the U.C. Berkeley Wellness letter, and asked for every possible test and benefit. The older black men tended to be less informed and less assertive.

At the meeting, a guideline was proposed that recommended ordering the PSA test for the patients who asked for it (that patient satisfaction piece), but not mentioning it to patients who didn't bring it up. I knew how that would work out in my practice. The white men, at lower risk, would be tested, and the black men, at higher risk, would not. I spoke up and said that I was not comfortable with this recommendation, given the high rate of prostate cancer in the African-American community. I was outvoted, but I ignored the guideline in my practice. I offered the test to every man of the appropriate age.

I had been at Kaiser at least five years when a male colleague walked past my office just before lunch and announced, "I had a great morning. Two of my urgent care appointments didn't fill." Since I became a regular doctor, I had never had an urgent care slot go empty. That day, after work, I started cruising the schedules of other doctors on the computer. I had always looked only at mine. To my astonishment, there were male doctors who had as much as an hour of free time during the day, because there were no patients in four urgent care slots. I made a chart that looked at one time, 4:30, over several weeks, and could show that I always had a patient then, but there were colleagues who rarely did. I took it to the chief. She said, "The medical assistants know that you're such a good doctor."

No they didn't. They knew I was a black woman geriatrician, who spoke some Spanish. The slogan of the day was, "Give the patient what they want, when they want it". In a facility where the patients were mostly women and half black, many Spanish speaking and elderly, there would always be more patients requesting me than my white male colleagues. I would never get a break. The chief said that she would try to speak to the people on the telephone. Although the computers could track every prescription we wrote, she claimed there was no way for the computer to keep track of how many urgent care appointments each doctor had.

I repeated the survey a few months later, and nothing had changed. This time I had a plan. I had learned that one of the gynecologists at our facility inserted vacation time into his schedule in 15 minute pieces, to give himself time to return phone calls and go to the bathroom. I offered to use my vacation time in the same way, fifteen minutes morning and afternoon. The chief refused. "It wouldn't be fair," she said.

When I talked to women colleagues who also routinely had more appointments than the men did, they told me to stop looking at other people's schedules if it upset me. They didn't dispute my findings—some of them had noticed it themselves. They were resigned.

One Friday morning, two exam rooms were empty for fifteen minutes, although I had a full schedule. That never happened, so I walked up front to find the MA. She was on the phone, hunched over the counter so she couldn't see me. I spoke her name, and when she didn't respond, I tapped her on the shoulder to show her the charts of patients who had registered : three were waiting. I thought a tap was more discrete than yelling at her to get her attention. I went back to my office, and she went to the station manager and accused me of assault. A touch in the workplace is an assault, if an employee chooses to lodge a complaint. I learned later that medical assistant was already on probation, so I imagine that she figured she'd better go after me to prevent me from complaining about her.

I gave a statement to the police that day. The following week, the threat committee from the regional office, the same people who investigate bomb threats, came and talked to everyone at my station. In the end (weeks) they exonerated me: their official conclusion was that no assault had occurred. But, my chief warned me, "people" thought I was angry, and if there were another incident, I would be fired.

The next few months I had intrusive thoughts, flashbacks, insomnia. "People" were right. I was angry, and I had been angry for years. At meetings, in memos, the company urged us to provide better customer service, not to keep patients waiting. I should have cared less, I should have stayed in my office, waited until the MA brought the patients, however late. This was what Lorraine meant, "Don't get involved." Why was I so impossibly naïve, about my office mate, about the schedule, about employee relations?

A colleague (without children), hearing my story, confided that she had been caught padding her schedule with dead patients to get a break during the day. She looked at me wild-eyed and said "If I don't get out of here, I am going to kill someone or kill myself." (She transferred to another facility.) I felt the same desperation. I was afraid to leave Kaiser because I remembered how difficult private practice was. Yet I was afraid to stay. I couldn't be sure that I wouldn't unconsciously tap someone on the shoulder again.

When I left Kaiser, my colleagues gave me a party and a Dilbert cartoon book that they had inscribed. Those were indeed the Dilbert years. Lorraine says that it takes about a year to get Kaiser programming out of your system. I felt guilty, for letting down my beleaguered colleagues. I moved on to a job at Summit hospital, in the medical community where I had started out. The hospitals had merged, and many colleagues had left, but it still felt like a homecoming. I joined a group of doctors who contracted with the hospital to provide care for the uninsured, and cared for many of the patients of private doctors who no longer wanted to do hospital work. I was part of a new trend, internists who work only in the hospital, called hospitalists. Although I had walked away from my last, best chance to have my own practice, I knew I had made the right decision when my ten year old daughter said to me, "I like your new job better, Mom. You used to come home tired and angry, but now you're just tired."

At first, I enjoyed the physical freedom and adrenalin of the work. I loved roaming the halls of the hospital, moving from floor to floor, after years in one corner of one station all day. It made a huge psychological difference to control when I saw the patient, rather than waiting for them to show up. At Kaiser, if a patient showed up anytime during a clinic period, they had to be seen. So the nine a.m. patient who came at eleven had to be worked in somehow.

I loved being able to consult with colleagues face-to-face again, and truly feeling part of a team, with nurses who had the patient's welfare at heart. But everyone was still overworked, and the winter flu season found us constantly triaging patients, discharging those who were halfway stable in order to open beds for the people waiting in the emergency room who were more desperately ill. There were only three hospitals left in Oakland: Summit, Kaiser and the county hospital, Highland. Often only one hospital was open to ambulances, because the other two were full: we took turns "on diversion."

I found myself wondering why I always had to deliver care at ninety miles an hour, no matter what the setting. I don't know the answer. But after five years at Summit, I decided to work a minimal schedule, not seven tenths and hospital call as I had at Kaiser, not five or six days in a row as I did as a hospitalist, but two days of disability consultation (chart review) at the Social Security Administration and half day of clinic a week. I have two weekdays to write, an incredible luxury. I have made peace with my split doctor/writer identity and no longer berate myself for not pursuing a more serious medical career or not having the guts to walk away from medicine and write full time.

I left private practice in 1988; Judith hung on for another decade. During those years, internists in private practice in the Bay Area faced unrelenting change. Judith didn't change jobs, but her job changed beneath her. In San Francisco, where she practiced, four hospitals, Pacific Presbyterian, Children's, RK Davies and Marshal Hale, merged into one, owned by Sutter Health. Judith trained and practiced at Children's Hospital, founded around the turn of the last century by women doctors who were denied privileges at the more upscale Pacific Presbyterian. Women remained in control of the board of directors at Children's, and over the years, Asian doctors found Children's Hospital more welcoming to their patients. So the merger of the two medical staffs was a cross-cultural marriage, with all the stress of such a union.

Health care planners talked about the market forces that precipitated the mergers, how they were necessary to get rid of excess bed capacity and achieve economies of scale. On the ground, mergers mean lay-offs and low morale. Doctors who thought they avoided corporate medicine by choosing private practice rather than Kaiser generally did not rush to embrace Sutter Health. The new hospital paid some doctors to help select the chiefs of the various medical departments. Until Judith protested, none of these committees included women doctors. She was told the omission was an "oversight", an echo of the way I had been "overlooked" on the medical staff years earlier. After Judith spoke up, she and another woman physician were appointed to selection committees.

In the office, financial worries dominated Judith's concerns. The new HMOs competed to see "how low can we go" in physician reimbursements. Blue Cross even imposed a "handling fee" for processing claims until the state legislature outlawed it. It took up to six months for them to pay a claim. MediCal used to simply "suspend" payment when the state ran out of money, as though doctors could "suspend" staff salaries. The practice gross income looked okay, partly because everyone was working more hours, but Judith's net income kept dropping, Meanwhile, the bookkeeper visited the ATM twice a day, his wife stopped working, he owned three cars, one a Lexus, and he and his wife lived in the largest unit of an eight unit apartment building he owned.

By 1993, enough primary care doctors were leaving San Francisco, either to join Kaiser or leave the area, that the new hospital, California Pacific Medical Center, decided to offer management support services to primary care physicians. Judith's practice of five doctors signed on for an audit, in hopes of improving their efficiency, and learned that their bookkeeper had been stealing their money.

Judith had her suspicions earlier, and it turned out that the office manager had discovered the crime two years prior to the audit, but she kept quiet because the bookkeeper had threatened to kill her.

Judith's lawyer husband, Bob, came into the office the Friday afternoon that the five doctors confronted the bookkeeper. The meeting with the doctors, Bob and the bookkeepers took place in her consulting office for privacy. When everyone had squeezed in, Bob spoke. "We want you to authorize the bank to let us review your account activity over the last three years. We are going to press charges, but if you allow us access, the court will be more lenient with you." Three years was the statute of limitation for embezzlement.

The bookkeeper hung his head and asked for the weekend to think it over.

Bob and the doctors argued in front of the bookkeeper whether to give him the weekend. A couple of the doctors felt that he had been a reliable employee, even though he had been stealing. In the end, they agreed to meet with him on Monday, but they placed bets as to whether he would show up. He did.

Bob looked at all the bank records and discovered that the bookkeeper was grossing about $150,000 more than his $48,000 salary each year.

One out of three doctors' offices discover an employee with hands in the till. Doctors are easy marks, because they are busy coping with their patients, and assume loyalty that isn't there. I know this, because the office manager in my husband's office stole from them during the same years Judith's bookkeeper took her money. Both employees skimmed off the cash that patients gave for their co-payments. (Hence all the ATM visits.) The co-pays represented the low-lying fruit. Then they wrote checks to themselves on the office account, or deposited receipts in their own accounts. Both embezzlers explained away lower net income in the practices by blaming managed care.

My husband Miles discovered the problem when the office manager went on maternity leave, and the accountant told him to put aside ten percent of the practice income for refunds to insurance companies. Miles, concerned that the billing was very inaccurate if they had to refund ten percent of their gross income each month, checked the bank statements that the accountant never saw. The accountant balanced the checkbook using the information the office manager wrote on the check stubs. She had instructed the bank to keep the actual checks, which were written to her Mercedes Benz dealer, her son, and her bank account, not insurance companies.

Bob helped Judith her build the case against her bookkeeper, but they could only prove that he took $320,000 over three years. They estimated that the total was $700,000. In my husband's three person gastroenterology practice, where the doctors all performed procedures, the figure was two million dollars over six years. Judith and I both remember endless lawyer meetings in our "free" time.

Judith's practice sued both the bookkeeper and the banks that should have noticed that something was amiss. They recovered $60,000 from the banks, and worked out a payment plan with the bookkeeper, but he has only complied with a fraction of the court-ordered payments. He did spend 6 days in jail, which is unusual for a white collar criminal.

On our side of the bay, we sued the accountants and the office manager, but she was married to one of the partners during the years of the embezzlement. If we had nailed her to the wall, we would have bankrupted my husband's partner, who denied all knowledge of her theft. My husband and the founding partner elected to keep the partnership together. The marriage was annulled, and she eventually did a few months of jail time, but we only recovered a few thousand dollars from the accountants.

One of the highlights of Judith's practice life was the opportunity to found and direct a small inpatient eating disorders unit for five years. She recognized from the beginning that it was not a smart financial move for her. The hospital paid her $24,000 a year for what was supposed to be a half-time position and spilled into much more. But, she says, she loved the opportunity to do things right for once, to have enough nutrition and psychiatric and nursing support for these challenging patients. After years of running herself ragged to get it up and going, she handed the unit over to another physician, who directed it for another year or so, until it, too, fell a victim to cost-cutting.

While she was in private practice, Judith continued to do clinical teaching and give nutrition lectures at the medical school (unpaid, of course). She was the only woman on the Board of Directors of the Bay Pacific HMO, until it disbanded in 2000. In that position, she did receive stock shares, and about $100 a month. More recently, she was appointed to the California Commission on Aging, which meets for two days every six weeks or so.

My children use the expression "Where's the juice?" to ask where is the part that is close to your heart, that keeps you going. When Judith was in private practice, the professional activities that didn't add much if anything to her bottom line were the juice for her. Of course, there are always wonderful patients who make a doctor's day, but Judith often felt ground down by the expectations of the affluent women in her practice. If we general doctors cared only about money, we would have been specialists. On the other hand, as Judith puts it, "I didn't like the assumption that as a woman, I should always spend more time, always give more. And if I didn't, their level of disappointment astonished me."

The additional pressure from direct-to-patient advertising was a particular trial in private practice, because every insurance company paid for different medications. Often they covered only a few drugs in each class, which made sense, because many medications are very similar and equally effective. For example, the anti-depressants may differ in their side effect profile, and some people may respond better to one than another, but in general, they all work. The clinician wants to prescribe a drug he knows well and one that is on the formulary. The patient wants the pill he heard about on T.V.

In order to help her cope with high patient expectations of accessibility, Judith paid for a half-time RN, a practice expense that she did not share with her partners. The nurse's salary ate into her income, but it was worth it to her to relieve some of the daily burden of messages. She found, just as I had at Kaiser, that the medical assistants didn't have enough training to ease the burden of call-backs and prescription refills. They don't understand enough medicine, especially in a general practice, where the range of prescriptions is infinite, unlike, for example, a gynecologist's practice.

Unfortunately, the nurse Judith hired turned out to have substance abuse issues. One Monday morning, Judith took a call from a pharmacist who asked her if her RN was authorized to call in Vicodin prescriptions in Judith's name on the weekend. Of course not. So Judith called the five or six pharmacies they generally used, and found that the nurse had been prescribing Vicodin in Judith's name to fictitious patients. Judith called the nurse into her office and confronted her with the evidence. She tearfully admitted that she was addicted to Vicodin. Judith gave her two months severance pay and paid for $1000 of her diversion treatment.

A year later, Judith closed her private practice and took a three day a week salaried job at the newly created Institute for Health and Healing. The nurse episode is one of the straws that broke the camel's back.

Over the last five years that she was in private practice, Judith's net income declined every year, to the point that she was making $68,000 a year, less than a nurse with comparable experience. Maybe she wasn't the world's best businesswoman, but she worked the same fifty to sixty hours a week each year. More than any of us, Judith believed in the ideal of the doctor who cares for the whole person. When we were medical students, she gave each of us in the group a copy of *Doctor Nellie,* the autobiography of Helen MacKnight Doyle, 1873-1957, who was a pioneer California doctor. Originally published in 1934, it's a period piece, but Dr. Nellie's plucky prose was a balm when we needed it. Here is how Doyle describes meeting her doctor husband, "I had worked so long, fighting my way against the criticism and scorn of the other physicians of the town, that it seemed a wonderful thing to find a man who believed in me and was willing to work with me to the common end of the greatest good to the patient." That's Judith, working for the greatest good of the patient.

The Institute for Health and Healing at California Pacific Medical Center is a center for combined Western and alternative therapy modalities. They offer chiropractic, Ayurvedic medicine, massage therapy, acupuncture and biofeedback. Judith does evaluations of patients with medical and nutritional issues, often cancer patients, or patients with eating disorders. She does not take over the primary care of these patients, but sends a detailed letter back to the regular doctor with her recommendations. The patients pay out of pocket for her one and a half hour consultation, then seek reimbursement, if possible, from their insurance company. Obviously, she still serves an affluent clientele. But now she can listen long enough to satisfy them, and she doesn't have the ongoing responsibility for their care. She's a specialist.

Judith has served in her new role for almost five years now, and she is much happier. Yet even as she basks in the sunshine, the storm clouds are massing. A year ago, the medical center, which had subsidized the various practitioners by paying their overhead and their salaries, decided to withdraw their financial support. Everyone has to pay their own rent and staff expenses, do their own billing, and pay themselves: a private practice model. It is not clear how many of the individual practitioners in the Institute will survive, even on their wealthy island, and whether Judith will be one of them. If not, she has decided to retire, rather than reinvent herself in another physician role. She's in her early sixties, her children are out of college, and she's had a good run.

11. The Microenvironment

"It is perfectly evident from the records, that the opposition to women physicians has rarely been based upon any sincere conviction that women could not be instructed in medicine, but upon an intense dislike to the idea that they should be so capable." (Mary Putnam Jacobi, MD, *Woman's Work in America*, 1864)

Many years ago, my little niece had a persistent case of eczema. She woke up in the night itching, and then woke my sister Carol, her mother. Neither of them was getting enough sleep, and despite Carol's constant admonitions, "Don't scratch, don't scratch," my niece had long scars. I urged Carol to call Lorraine for advice. Carol was reluctant to bother Lorraine because her daughter had already seen several dermatologists. She had prescription cream and anti-itching pills. What else was there to do? Frankly, I didn't know, but I had confidence that Lorraine would. Finally, my sister made the call. Lorraine asked, "Have you tried Vaseline?" Carol slathered her daughter with Vaseline that evening and the child slept through the night for the first time in a month.

Lorraine is curious about everything, especially topics that bother her patients but other academics might consider mundane. She is also relentlessly pragmatic, which is unusual for an academic doctor. She has not forgotten her years at Kaiser. I have heard her diaper rash lecture, and it is a masterful synthesis of the medical research and the concerns of patients.

In another example of pragmatism, Lorraine spoke out against the American Academy of Pediatrics guidelines for the use of sunscreen in children. Since sunscreen hadn't been tested in babies less than a year old, the AAP had advised against sunscreen and suggested that mothers keep their children indoors for the first six months.

"You can't say that to mothers," Lorraine objected. "You'll just make them feel guilty when they have to take the baby along to the sibling's soccer game or the family reunion picnic. We can talk about minimizing sun exposure, about hats and long sleeves. But we can't say keep them indoors." The guidelines recently changed.

After leaving the Permanente Group, Lorraine developed a theory about what makes a job comfortable. "It's not the macro environment that's important on a job. I recognize that in many ways, the Kaiser system is a progressive force in health care. It was my microenvironment, the people I worked with on a day-to-day basis and the politics of our local facility that made me leave." When she arrived at UCSF, Lorraine found a more welcoming microenvironment, starting with the chief who hired her, and offered her paid maternity leave before she had been there a year. "When I interviewed, I asked the chief if he was thinking about leaving. I knew that he was fair and wanted me to succeed. And by then, I'd had enough experience with institutional politics to know how important that attitude was." He assured her that he would stay. He did end up leaving after five years, but by then Lorraine was established and able to hold her own.

The other pediatric dermatologist in the department, a woman who had been Lorraine's resident when she was a third-year student on pediatrics, wanted to spend more time in the lab doing research. She had built the reputation of the fledgling subspecialty by herself, and was happy to have a colleague to share the clinical load. "I couldn't have asked for a more generous colleague. I never felt that we were in competition."

Finally, just before Lorraine joined the department, the dermatologists had bought one of the new lasers developed for use on the skin. At other medical centers, pediatric dermatologists were starting to use lasers to remove the congenital birthmarks on the face called port wine stains. Often these "stains" covered half the face, and unlike some other birthmarks, did not go away as the child matured. Lorraine was in the right place at the right time to learn to use the laser for children. After years in practice, she approached learning this procedure with confidence that she hadn't had as a third-year student. Like all procedures, it is more lucrative than seeing patients, so in a sense, her laser work helps finance some of her clinical work that doesn't generate income for the clinic.

Lorraine points to the vascular anomalies clinic that she cofounded in 1990 with an interventional radiologist and a plastic surgeon as an example of the kind of work that she feels is important, because it is a better way to care for patients. When parents bring in a baby with a birthmark that involves arteries and veins, the best treatment is often not clear. All invasive options are tricky because of the risk of bleeding. In the vascular anomaly clinic, the specialists (now including other surgical specialties as well as an RN coordinator) can discuss the case at one sitting. This way parents don't have to run from one department to another getting different and often contradictory opinions. It's the equivalent of a tumor board for cancer patients.

Again, Lorraine's chief was farsighted enough to support the establishment of the clinic, even though it did not make money. (Insurance companies don't care how many specialists are in the room. For them, it's one clinic visit.) After almost fifteen years, the existence of the clinic has enhanced the reputation of the department and provided an unusual learning opportunity for the residents of the many specialties involved. There is a parallel here with the eating disorders unit that Judith founded: both Lorraine and Judith recognized that a collaborative approach would best serve the patients and their families. The difference in the fate of the two programs reflects the fact that outside of a teaching setting, an initiative that doesn't make or save money will not survive, no matter how much it benefits the patient.

Lorraine says that when she was growing up, she never felt that she had a special talent, unlike her older sister who danced and her younger sister who is an artist. She has a good eye for patterns on the skin and the scholarship to give meaning to her observations. She feels that she found her talent in pediatric dermatology, and the recognition that she receives is all the more special because she never expected it. (Although Lorraine is the only one of us to achieve national prominence in her field, we all feel that we have succeeded beyond our expectations, partly because our expectations were so low.)

Like all of us, Lorraine tries to address the emotion behind the visit, as well as the physical problem, because she knows that satisfying the patient means figuring out that emotion, even if it's not expressed. Many times, mothers who come to her are reluctant to use the mild hydrocortisone cream that the pediatrician has prescribed for fear of "steroid side effects." Lorraine spends time discussing those fears, trying to put them in context, because she knows that the treatment failed not because it was wrong, but because it wasn't used. As the expert, she can also assure the anxious mothers that the pediatrician is not withholding a magical salve without side effects.

Lorraine feels lucky that she has not faced the political barriers in her academic career that other women have encountered. There are many women in both pediatrics and dermatology, and her mentor was one of the first doctors to specialize in pediatric dermatology. Recently, there was some confusion about whether Lorraine was a candidate for a more prestigious academic track: a rumor reached her that a colleague had said that Lorraine was not interested. She immediately clarified her interest via email, and was assured that no one had ever doubted that she wanted the promotion. On the other hand, no one had mentioned that the supporting letters were due the following week, until she emailed. Lorraine cites this incident as a reminder that people should not expect that they will receive what they deserve without asking for it, a lesson we women learn over and over.

After Sam's Hodgkin's Disease, Lorraine's concern for him swamped any anxiety she had about her own health, leaving her less fixated on her own mortality. For once, her loved one didn't die. "Intellectually, I knew that people didn't always die of cancer. But emotionally, I didn't believe it." When she was called back for an abnormal mammogram (false alarm) shortly after Sam's treatment, all she could think was, "I don't have time for cancer right now." She has research goals that she would like to achieve before she steps down and looks forward to a time when she can devote some of the mental energy she now spends keeping one step ahead of her teenagers, to her work.

The juice for Lorraine in her work is in her research and the mentoring of residents and junior faculty. She was instrumental in assembling an investigative group at seven medical centers to study hemangiomas. She describes it as an effort based on passion and optimism: it, too, was initially unfunded. It is a detailed cohort study of children with blood vessel tumors. They managed to enroll a thousand patients in fifteen months, a remarkable feat in the world of clinical research, where most investigators struggle to find enough patients willing to participate. Recently, they received a large grant to do data analysis. As it happens, the lead investigator at each of the institutions is a woman. Privately, they call themselves the Hemangioma Girls Club.

In contrast to Lorraine, when Ruth left Kaiser, she did not find a warmer microenvironment. She went from being a well-respected, salaried specialist in a system where she never lacked for patients, to an unknown partner in a multi-specialty group where she had to build a practice and pay overhead from day one. There were three gastroenterologists in the nine-person practice, five general internists, one cardiologist, and one endocrinologist.

The senior gastroenterologist had recruited her, so Ruth assumed that both gastroenterologists were busy. It turned out that although they wanted someone else to share the overhead, the younger gastroenterologist was still building his practice, too, so he and Ruth competed for referrals. It would have been a difficult situation for anyone to walk into, but for Ruth, who is internally driven to be the best, it was a particular trial. "My ego was destroyed. No one knew me, no one knew how good I was. I was an anonymous doctor doing HMO physicals." As someone who has done my share of HMO physicals, I can imagine worse, but it was quite a comedown for a specialist.

As Ruth talks about the early days of her private practice, I think back to a dinner meeting we girls had back then. I remember that it was almost impossible to find a date when we could all attend. We finally settled on a weeknight and chose a restaurant near Ruth's office in San Francisco, because she said she couldn't get far. The restaurant wasn't particularly fancy, but I was still somewhat surprised when Ruth showed up in her scrub suit. Now it makes more sense. She was working so hard, she could barely get out of the office to see us.

At first, Ruth did more general internal medicine to pay the bills, while she was establishing her reputation as a gastroenterologist. She estimates that she spent 80 percent of her time in the office and 20 percent doing procedures. Now that ratio is almost reversed. She spends 70 percent of her time doing procedures, mostly colonoscopies, and 30 percent in the office. Once the other doctors started to refer to her, Ruth was able to capitalize on her position as the only female gastroenterologist in her medical community. She sees the patients who won't have a colonoscopy unless they can have a woman doctor, who tend to be an anxious group. Like Judith, she feels that patients assume she will be more accommodating because she is a woman, but in her specialist role she can do the procedure and send the patient back to the general internist.

The advent of the screening colonoscopy changed every gastroenterologist's life, including those of Ruth and my husband. Until the last few years, the sigmoidoscopy was the procedure of choice for colon cancer screening. Both procedures involve inserting a tube up the rectum to look at the bowel, but the sigmoidoscopy is an examination of the left side of the colon, the sigmoid colon, while the colonoscopy is an examination of the whole colon. Since the sigmoidoscope is shorter and less difficult to maneuver, many general doctors, like myself, were trained to use them. (The risk of tearing the colon is one in ten thousand for sigmoidoscopy, one in one thousand for colonoscopy.) In fact, at Kaiser, registered nurses perform sigmoidoscopies. Patients were referred to a GI specialist only if there was a suspicious growth, a polyp, which required a biopsy. At that time, the gastroenterologist would perform a colonoscopy to make sure there were no polyps in the two-thirds of the colon beyond the reach of the sigmoidoscope.

Then Katie Couric, the TV personality, had a screening colonoscopy with the cameras rolling. Her husband had died of colon cancer, and she wanted to encourage people to be screened. Boy, did she ever. In response to the publicity she generated, Medicare decided to pay for screening colonoscopies, and most of the private insurance companies followed Medicare's lead. There are not enough gastroenterologists in the country to screen every person over age fifty with a colonoscopy, which is the current recommendation.

There is still some debate about whether such an expensive, invasive test is really necessary, but well-informed patients have jumped on the bandwagon. Even though Medicare and private insurance companies pay less per procedure than they did ten years ago, the gastroenterologists do so many more of them that their income has increased. Another test, the "virtual colonoscopy" is under development, so it is not clear how long this bonanza will last, but for now, gastroenterologists are very busy. And they worship Katie Couric.

Ruth says that it took her five years to get on her feet in private practice and pay back the money she had borrowed from her husband's retirement plan to start out. Now she says that she has achieved everything she ever wanted professionally, and she is not looking for new horizons. She estimates that she reached a plateau close to age fifty. It is probably not coincidental that about the same time she had a significant health scare herself. While lifting weights at the gym, she noticed a painless lump in her neck.

Again, we are gathered in my living room listening attentively to Ruth's story, anxious to catch the details. The daylight is fading, but no one interrupts her to turn on the lights. After she says the word "gym" she pauses and laughs at the surprise on our faces. It is hard for us to imagine Ruth, a reluctant exerciser, at a gym.

"I only lasted a few months," she assures us. "At first, I thought I had strained something and developed a cyst. The lump was perfectly smooth, but it didn't go away. I was too busy to deal with it."

Exactly what Lorraine had said about her false positive mammogram.

"After a few months, I stopped the endocrinologist in our practice in the hall, and asked him to feel my neck. He thought it was probably a cyst, but he felt a little something on the other side, so he suggested a fine needle aspiration to make the diagnosis. We had Kaiser insurance (through her husband David), but I wasn't willing to take time off from work to go to an appointment elsewhere, so I paid $3,000 out of pocket for this guy to stick a needle in my neck. Over and over."

When the pathology report came back, it was non-diagnostic. Her colleague then suggested a nuclear medicine scan, which she had at her hospital ($2,000) so she could squeeze it in between procedures. The scan showed that the nodules were cold; in other words, they did not pick up the radioactive iodine tracer, as functioning thyroid tissue would. Looked like cancer.

The next day, David called her office, canceled her patients, and drove her across the Bay Bridge to his Kaiser facility. There, the endocrinologist hit the nodule on the first try, and pathology read out the diagnosis by noon. She had encapsulated papillary carcinoma of the thyroid. It was seven months after she first felt the lump.

"I think I knew on some level that no one dies of thyroid cancer. I had surgery, and radiation for good measure, and I'm fine. Five years without a problem. But it showed me how crazy I was, working like a mad woman."

"How did David take it?" I ask.

"You know, that's something. I think of him as the rock of our family, nothing gets to him. But he looked truly shaken when they gave us the diagnosis. He pulled strings to get the surgery scheduled for the next day."

Ruth was in a pensive mood that day. Her father had died a few months earlier, and she had just returned from her older son's college orientation.

"I wish I had been able to do things differently, that I wasn't so driven. It all goes so fast."

I knew that Lorraine, sitting next to Ruth on the couch, facing high school with the twins, was thinking, it can't go fast enough for me. Lorraine is on top of the world professionally and feels right now that her teenagers are the weights that keep her from flying.

"Oh, I don't know," Judith says. "My boys are independent and confident."

"No, that's not what she means." I speak because this subject has been much on my mind. "The kids are fine. Everyone told us that the kids would suffer, but we worked so hard, at home, too, that the kids are fine. It's us. What we missed."

Ruth nods.

Lorraine asks Ruth, "What's fun for you about your work now?"

At first Ruth says ruefully, "Well, when I'm on my tenth colonoscopy of the day, there's not a lot about my job that looks fun." But she thinks a minute, and says, "The good people."

We must look puzzled, because she continues, "Sure, the entitled, self-absorbed, demanding patients eat up our time." We groan.

"But there are people who are so loving and generous. Like Mrs. X (a name we all recognize), who used her money to take AIDS patients to Paris. She died this year, and I was devastated."

A few days later, when I called Karen in Los Angeles, to hear her part of the conversation, I tried to convey the mood in the room, as I always do when she can't be with us. She had two big life events herself that year, her youngest daughter's Bat Mitzvah and the birth of her first grandchild. She's not crazy about how old being a grandparent makes her feel. "It's been worse for Frank, because he's the biological grandparent. As the stepmother, I can let people assume I'm much younger." On the other hand, she's glad that she had room in her schedule to help the new mother.

Karen started doing evaluations for workers' compensation in 1991. She was renting office space for her private practice from a psychiatrist who did the exams, and he asked her to help out when he was busy. She found that she enjoyed the work, and decided to start her own workers' compensation practice because the overflow from her colleague was not a steady source of patients. Frank, who had experience with the dental clinics, helped her on the business side, especially the initial marketing to insurance companies. In the days before the state legislature instituted reforms, doctors lobbied the claims adjusters for business the way pharmaceutical representatives detail doctors. Karen says that she would have been more hesitant to make the move to her own office if Frank hadn't helped her; it would have been difficult for her to see patients and visit prospective clients at the same time. At one point she worked out of three different offices in three communities, but in the last few years she has cut back to one office near her home.

Workers' compensation evaluations are a specialized area of psychiatry. Karen sees patients for the insurance companies of employers. The patients tend to fall into one of three categories: bank tellers or others involved in holdups, who have post-traumatic stress disorder, people with physical injuries who are not getting better, like the "failed backs,"(patients still in pain after multiple surgeries), and in a grayer, more litigated area, people who claim harassment on the job, sexual or otherwise. Karen's job is to interview the patient, get the story, and give an opinion as to how impaired the patient is, in terms of "work functions." These include abilities like following instructions, working without supervision, concentrating.

If the patient doesn't have a treating doctor (many of them do) and she and the patient click, she can become the treating doctor. She estimates that 60 percent of her work is evaluations and 40 percent is treatment. Karen mostly supervises the medication end of treatment: she employs a non-MD therapist to help her with the rest. She likes the variety of the work and the fact that many of her patients would not ordinarily see a psychiatrist. A private psychiatric practice tends to be top-heavy with affluent neurotic patients. Her office is all women: Karen, the therapist, and the secretarial staff. When she attends conferences in her subspecialty, however, she stands out. "I look around the room and there are hardly any other women doctors or lawyers." Although 30 percent of psychiatrists are women, Karen landed in a microenvironment where women are scarce.

She speculates that, like her, other women are intimidated by the salesmanship required to establish a foothold in the competitive market.

In 1993, the California State Legislature passed a law that doctors who contract with insurance companies for workers' compensation evaluations have to pass a certification examination and take continuing education in the field. Before then, Karen says, the field was rife with fraud and abuse. Doctors would give kickbacks to insurance company examiners for referrals. There are still doctors nicknamed "washout doctors" who will always deny the claim if the insurance company wants the claim denied. An examiner who reads many physician reports tends to have an idea what kind of opinion he'll get from which doctor after a while, but Karen says she doesn't worry about her next referral; she just tries to do what's fair.

Karen feels that one reason that she is well suited to this field is that she enjoys writing. She likes assembling the pieces of the story, some from the medical records, some from the patient, in a detailed report for the insurance company. She dictates the reports, but it feels like writing. Many doctors dislike writing (my husband always said that I entirely missed the point of taking science courses, which was to avoid writing essays), so I am not surprised that Karen says that the examiners praise her reports. I have had the same experience at the Social Security Administration, where I write analyses of disability cases.

Karen says that she has thought about retirement (Frank retired a few years ago), but she doesn't want to leave her niche yet. Her office manager is a close friend, and she has worked with all her employees for many years. She would miss the social aspects of the job as much as the work. Lorraine and Ruth also mentioned the importance of their work friendships. Lorraine works closely with an RN who "saves me every day, in every way." Ruth, who remembered most vividly the hostility of nurses when she was in training, now invites the nurses she works with in the GI lab to the second home her family shares in the country. They like to "hang out and drink."

I remember when I first started in practice how envious I was of the community the nurses had created. On the wards, in the hospital, the nurses organized potluck lunches on holidays or other special occasions. Sometimes I would be invited, because they asked doctors that they liked to sample their cooking, but they didn't invite me as a participant. In the beginning, I would try to contribute a dish. They would act surprised that I cooked, then say, "Oh, no, the doctors don't bring anything."

We have come full circle, now, the girls and I, because the nurses who intimidated us when we were students are our allies and friends in the struggle to provide health care in an environment that changes as quickly as a stage set. I think of the RN who helped me with the HIV patients at Kaiser. She is a natural healer, full of New Age optimism. "You're not having a bad day, you're having a challenging day, a day of growth," she would tell me on our lunchtime walks. Nurses don't play the role of "wives at work" for us, as they often do for male doctors, but now nurses are our girlfriends at work.

This is not an easy time for doctors, men or women. If we had been five men, the dermatologist and the gastroenterologist would still be the high earners, more invested in their careers. Everyone is running from primary care, and psychiatry has lost much of its prestige. The difference is that Judith, Karen, and I have high-earning husbands, so we don't have to keep slogging sixty hours a week. My own internist, in private practice, describes himself as "bitter." One study showed that more than half of internists our age are looking to cut down on patient care time. At Kaiser they talk about "the golden handcuffs," the retirement benefits that keep doctors working. The handcuffs don't fit women as well, because more of us can afford to slip out of them. All three of us who left took jobs that initially paid less. Judith was also able to hang on longer in private practice because she wasn't the sole support of her family.

Despite the greater numbers of women in medicine, the profession has been slow to examine our experience. A prominent professor in family practice told me that life was just hard in family practice, for men and women, so there was no point in talking about women separately. (I hear an echo, voices of black men in the seventies who wouldn't consider rights for women because nation-building came first.) The health policy people notice that we work fewer hours, which is attributed entirely to our role as mothers.

A few months after I left Kaiser, a friend reported that the new physician-in-chief came to her department meeting. A doctor asked him about low medical-staff morale. He wasn't worried. "No one ever really leaves Kaiser. Sometimes doctors transfer to a different facility, but no one leaves." With that one sentence, he erased the difficult decisions three of us had made, two at his medical center. A year or so later, a younger, childless woman on my station also left, to take a second residency in nuclear medicine, so I know that I wasn't the last one out the door. The point is not that some women leave. The point is that none of us left to stay home with the children.

12. Medicine Changed Us, But We Changed Medicine

"If we talk to the token woman lawyer, doctor, board member, tenured professor, we soon discover that she conceives herself not as an outsider but rather as an insider among men." (Carolyn Heilbrun, *Reinventing Womanhood*, 1979)

One evening at the clinic last year, we were an all-female staff: a nurse midwife who saw the pregnant patients and those with gynecological problems, two female medical assistants, and me, the internist. The medical assistant working with me told me that I had seen my last patient and that she and I could go home. It was close to nine p.m. and we were looking forward to dinner. On my way out, the other medical assistant stopped me. She asked if I would be willing to see one of the urgent care patients assigned to the midwife, who was behind schedule.

I hesitated, as I always do when I wonder whether a male doctor would have been asked the same favor. As an RN, a midwife is lower in the medical hierarchy than a doctor. ("Hell,no," my husband said when I asked him later. "And if he were asked, he wouldn't have done it," he added.) Patients and staff assume that I know more gynecology than I do, because I'm a woman. So I do more pelvic examinations than my male colleagues, and I read more about women's health, because I know I will be asked. I'm not alone. Women internists and family practitioners do twice as many pelvic exams as men do.

When my children were young, and I was anxious to get home, I would have resented this mild request. Before I understood and accepted my role as a "woman doctor," I would have been tempted to make the feminist point by saying "no," I would not help out. In fact, I said "yes," and saw the patient. Now that my children are grown and I have limited my clinical hours, it just doesn't make that much difference. Gender matters at work, but whether we perceive gender differences as a problem depends on the context.

Doctors tend to view the current status of women in medicine as the result of "a temporary representational lag." This is the "pipeline" metaphor: women will filter into all specialties and rise into positions of leadership when there are enough of us in the pipeline. We feminists would add that there have been structural barriers to the advancement of women doctors, but we are proud of the progress our generation made in dismantling them, particularly in training, and feel confident that the remaining barriers will yield to our forthright approach. Medicine changed us, but we have changed medicine.

The sociologist Elianne Riska points out that there is a third way to look at gender differences in the medical profession: not only as an artifact left over from past discrimination, not only as a result of structural barriers that are relatively easy to modify, but as a reflection of the gender inequality of the larger society. In our working lives, we women repeatedly bumped up against different expectations in the workplace: from colleagues, staff, patients, and ultimately ourselves. The earlier, pioneer, women doctors, avoided these expectations by embracing a stereotypical masculine identity. Frances Conley was tougher than the other boys.

In our generation, there were too many of us to blend in as "one of the boys" even if that had been our goal. We wanted to have the best of both worlds: the assertion and prestige of men, the communication skills and empathy of women. The doctors we admired combined these "masculine" and "feminine" characteristics. While we all can and do function as insiders among men, we have not lost sight of ourselves as women. There were enough of us that we could create a new way of being a doctor.

Today, although women represent a quarter of all doctors, the distribution of women in the landscape varies from specialty to specialty. In the citadel, the surgeons live on in the masculine culture that has lost its sway over the rest of medicine. The 10 percent of women in general surgery (3 or 4 percent in specialties like cardiovascular surgery and urology) still have to focus on crossing the moat and storming the gates to gain entrance. At the other extreme, in the happy valley of pediatrics, with equal numbers of men and women, the definition of a good doctor includes people skills. No one says, "He's such an acute diagnostician when our kids our sick, I don't care if he's a jerk" the way they say "He's such a good technician in the operating room, I don't care about his bedside manner." Between the citadel and the valley lies the vast plain in the middle, from anesthesia to ob-gyn to dermatology, but largely internal medicine and family practice, about a quarter women. There men and women doctors practice alongside each other, but not in the same way. The skirmishes between "masculine" and "feminine" values are out on the plains.

In the past, the waves of women who spread over the landscape tended to flow where there was least resistance, where our role was closest to our cultural role. Pediatrics, obstetrics, and gynecology are now considered "natural" fields for women, even though obstetricians are surgeons. People often say, when I tell them that I'm an internist, "Gee, I thought you were a pediatrician. I don't know why." I do.

Ophthalmologists and obstetricians both train for four years after medical school, and the eye doctors have a much easier lifestyle, yet only 14 percent of ophthalmologists are women compared to 35 percent of obstetricians. To some extent, women doctors are responding to market demands here, women patients who want women doctors. Yet even in pathology, where there are no live patients, Riska points out that there is a male/female division of labor. Men do more autopsies and women specialize in microscope work, examining more tissues of women and children.

In internal medicine, women care for a higher proportion of women and the poor. A 2004 perspective piece in *The Annals of Internal Medicine* entitled "When Most Doctors are Women: What Lies Ahead" quotes a woman doctor who calls women the "housewives" of internal medicine, "those who take responsibility for the profession's 'grunt work' in their careers as general internists. Many of the tasks performed in these roles are arduous or may lack prestige; some are even altruistic." In general surgery, women are "channeled" into breast surgery. Today, even in surgery, women medical students do not have to construct a woman doctor identity from scratch, the way we did. However, there are also enough women to allow the creation of gender stereotypes, a development we did not foresee.

In the battle of "nature" vs. "nurture," the feminists came down squarely in the "nurture" camp. This theory supported us as we faced the medical profession: we saw no reason that we couldn't learn to be doctors, even though none of us had grown up with such ambition, even though only Karen had majored in biology. Our success proves that we were right.

What we didn't anticipate, when we sought to strike a balance between the "masculine" and the "feminine" virtues, was that public opinion would swing so far back to the "nature" side of the ongoing discussion. Suddenly women were from Venus and men were from Mars. We have seen a resurgence of single sex education for children, catering to our "fundamental differences."

The five of us have all worked alongside men, all the time. We have been colleagues and comrades. In training, we cared for men and women patients, and that was our expectation of practice. We wanted to practice patient-centered medicine, but we didn't seek to become "empathy specialists"; we hoped all doctors would practice that way. It may be that our experience as "women doctors" will turn out to be limited to our generation. Certainly, all medical students now are explicitly trained in communication skills. Perhaps women medical students today, who feel as entitled to their seat in the class as their male classmates, can avoid "the good girl double bind." However, as long as women have a weaker status shield in society, women doctors will, too.

Looking back, certain themes stand out in our careers. First, how little encouragement we had during training. We were not the darling sons fulfilling the dreams of our parents; we were the uppity daughters pushing into a new role for women. We had to muscle our way in, establish our authority, over and over again. We were excluded from the automatic respect a male doctor receives. My daughter tells me that when she says that her parents are doctors, her friends ask, "Your mother, too?" Judith says that some new patients still address her by her first name without asking, although she addresses them by their last name. Would any patient take that liberty with a sixty-year-old man? (Okay, she doesn't look sixty. But still.)

Second, we all found men who could tolerate our careers, and we stuck with them. Lorraine, who has been married the shortest time, marked her twentieth anniversary this year. Some of us wanted more help at home on a daily chore basis than we received, but our husbands could see us both as women and as doctors. This set them apart from many men. Thank you, guys, for hanging in there with us.

Third, each of us handled childcare in a different way, but it was always an issue. Money helps and more money helps more. Every "career woman" who is a mother faces mixed messages from friends and family. Ambition is still unseemly in a woman. In the U.S., we don't support families the way other countries do, and the years with young children are always stressful, whether Mom is home all the time or not. We admit, when we were in the thick of it, we felt vulnerable to accusations that we were "gambling with our children's lives." I don't believe we were "gambling" because we all worked hard at home, too. But if we were gambling, we won. We won big.

Finally, we were politically naïve, both during training and in our careers. We started with the belief that hard work alone would bring rewards. We embraced the idea of teamwork without understanding that men on a team are always jockeying for position, lobbying the coach to be included in the starting lineup, trying to get more playing time. Then, because we felt on probation, because we didn't want to be seen as "whiners" or "needy," it took a long time to learn to stand up for ourselves. Overall, the health care system is so dysfunctional that even we have difficulty focusing on the separate concerns of women doctors. But as our numbers increase, our issues become the issues of the profession.

Much has changed. My women students have the active support and encouragement of their families. Men (and women) find them attractive and interesting rather than nerdy and intimidating. They understand much more about the politics of medicine than we did. Like the men, they frequently have a parent, sometimes a mother, who is a doctor. We have helped transform the training years, with formal mentoring programs, a new emphasis on physician wellness, and work limits for residents. Some of my students complain that they feel babied in the third year, that the faculty and house staff seem too concerned with the welfare of the students. Imagine.

As a generation, we rejected the idea that the "normal" person is a seventy-kilogram man. We insisted that we were as "normal" and worthy of study as men were, and we are proud that clinical research today reflects our concerns. Lorraine, who chose an academic career, has achieved rock-star status in pediatric dermatology, organizing international meetings where she receives standing ovations. She says, with a twinkle in her eye, "I am a very big fish in a very small pond." The rest of us, who elected to "just practice medicine," have found niches where we are comfortable and appreciated. It's all about the microenvironment.

The next patient still captivates us. Our white coats allow us to walk into a room, close the door, and listen to a stranger's innermost secrets. As a psychiatrist, Karen chose to stop there, exploring the deep mysteries of the brain and behavior. Lorraine examines the largest organ, the skin, which hides clues to disease in plain sight. We three internists probe deeply, touch the most intimate places. Yes, Karen and Lorraine had less night call, but Ruth, Judith, and I were addicted to the rush of caring for the sickest patients, of sharing the lives of people coping with profound physical challenges, of staring death in the face. I remember Karen's goal, to grapple with the big questions in life. We have all achieved that goal.

When I met with my medical students at the end of their third year, many of them were considering detours from the straight MD path. One woman had a job in a laboratory lined up and hoped to have a baby. One man was off to the School of Public Health in Berkeley. And one young man, the most traditional student of the bunch when I'd met him first year, was "just taking a year off." I smiled. When we girls were in training, a man who announced that he was "just taking a year off" would have been viewed like a nun who wanted a trial separation from Jesus. Lacking in vocation.

It's a whole new world out there, in every way. The students check assignments on the curriculum Web site, listen to lectures online, and use the computer to "virtually dissect" cadavers and later, to "virtually operate." UCSF pays men and women to allow beginning students to examine them, so none of the students hesitate for fear of causing a patient more distress. Students start and interrupt their studies when they feel like it, and travel to the ends of the earth. Men and women doctors leave practice for parenting or other pursuits: some of them return to the profession, others don't. We girls still don't understand the women who leave the profession permanently for motherhood, but we are tolerant. As Ruth puts it, "We killed ourselves so that they could have these choices."

The "we" Ruth refers to is not just the five of us, but all the women in our generation who entered the medical profession determined to offer all patients the same consideration and to open the door to the profession all the way for the women who came after us. Often in history it is not clear whether the members of a social movement recognized themselves, or whether the passage of time makes unrelated individuals appear to be a group. We girls may have been clueless in regards to the medical profession, but we always knew who had our back.

Bibliography

Barnett, Rosalind C. and Caryl Rivers. *Same Difference: How Gender Myths Are Hurting Our Relationships, Our Children and Our Jobs.* Oshkosh, WI: Basic Books, 2004.

Bateson, Mary Catherine. *Composing a Life.* New York: Grove-Atlantic, 2001.

Braustein, Peter and Michael William Doyle, eds. *Imagine Nation: The American Counterculture of the 1960s and '70s.* New York : Routledge, 2002.

Cartwright, Lillian K. "Women in Medicine." PhD thesis in Psychology, UC Berkeley, 1969.

Chetkovich, Carol. *Real Heat: Gender and Race in the Urban Fire Service.* Piscataway, NJ: Rutgers University Press, 1997.

Chin, Eliza Lo, ed. *This Side of Doctoring: Reflections from Women in Medicine.* Thousand Oaks, CA: Sage Publications, 2002.

Conley, Frances K. *Walking Out on the Boys.* New York: Farrar, Straus and Giroux, 1998.

Doyle, Helen M. *Doctor Nellie.* Mammoth Lakes, CA: Genny Smith Books, 1983.

Etzkowitz, Henry, Carol Kemelgor, and Brian Uzzi. *Athena Unbound: The Advancement of Women in Science and Technology.* Cambridge: Cambridge University Press, 2000.

Fels, Anna. *Necessary Dreams: Ambition in Women's Changing Lives.* New York: Pantheon Books, 2004.

Fine, Cordelia. *A Mind of Its Own: How Your Brain Distorts and Deceives.* New York: W.W. Norton and Company, 2006.

Frum, David. *How We Got Here: The '70s: The Decade That Brought You Modern Life (For Better or For Worse)*. Oshkosh, WI: Basic Books, 2000.

Heilbrun, Carolyn G. *Reinventing Womanhood.* New York: W.W. Norton & Company, 1979.

Heilbrun, Carolyn G. *Writing a Woman's Life.* NewYork: W.W. Norton and Company, 1988.

Kaltreider, Nancy, ed. *Dilemmas of a Double Life: Women Balancing Careers and Relationships.* Lanham, MD: Jason Aronson Publisher, Gender in Crisis Series, 1997.

Levinson W, Lurie N. "When Most Doctors are Women: What Lies Ahead" *Ann Int Med.* 2004:141:471-474

Marks, Lara V. *Sexual Chemistry: A History of the Contraceptive Pill.* New Haven: Yale University Press, 2001.

Martin, Toni. *How to Survive Medical School.* New York: Holt, Rinehart and Winston, 1983.

Moldow, Gloria. *Women Doctors in Gilded-Age Washington: Race, Gender and Professionalization.* Champaign, IL: University of Illinois Press, 1987.

Morantz-Sanchez, Regina Markell. *Sympathy and Science: Women Physicians in American Medicine.* New York : Oxford University Press, 1985.

More, Ellen S. *Restoring the Balance: Women Physicians and the Profession of Medicine, 1850-1995.* Cambridge, MA: Harvard University Press, 1999.

Pellegrini, Fabio et al. "Role of Organizational Factors in Poor Blood Pressure Control in Patients with Type 2 Diabetes" *Arch Intern Med.* 2003;163:473-480

Riska, Elianne. *Medical Careers and Feminist Agendas: American, Scandinavian and Russian Women Physicians.* Berlin: Aldine de Gruyter, 2001.

Roiphe, Anne. *Fruitful.* Boston: Houghton Mifflin Company, 1996.

Schmittdiel, J et al. "Effect of Physician and Patient Gender Concordance on Patient Satisfaction and Preventive Care Practices"*J Gen Intern Med.* 2000;15:761-769

Schulman, Bruce J. *The Seventies:The Great Shift in American Culture, Society andPolitics.* New York: Free Press, 2001.

Walsh, Elsa. *Divided Lives: The Public and Private Struggles of 3 Accomplished Women.* New York: Simon and Shuster, 1995.

Weintraub, Arlene. "Robert Swanson and Herbert Boyer: Giving Birth to Biotech," *Business Week,* October 18, 2004.

Index

978-0-595-48726-
0-595-48726-2

25594923R00111

Made in the USA
San Bernardino, CA
04 November 2015